eco~logical archi-techture

Bioclimatic trends and Landscape Architecture in the Year 2001

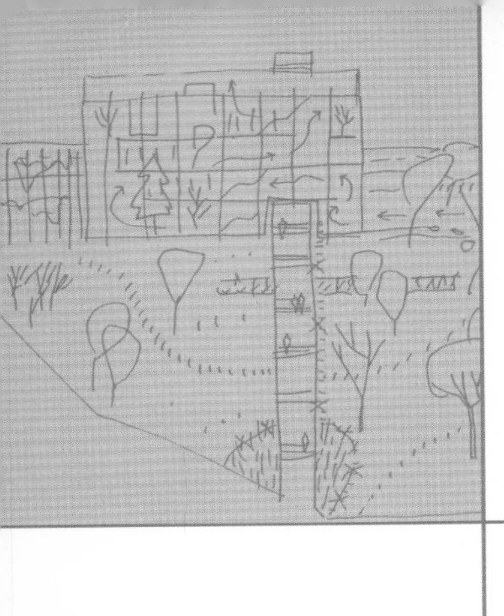

Publisher

Paco Asensio

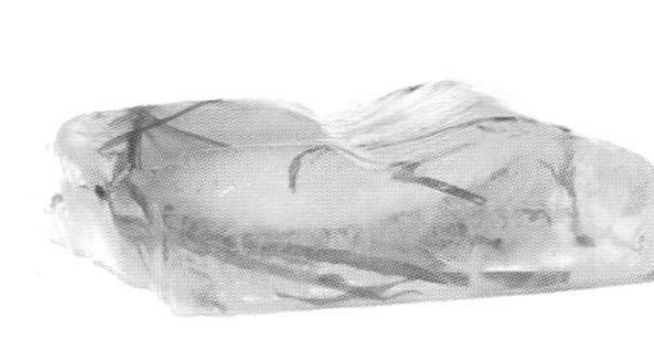

Editor

Aurora Cuito

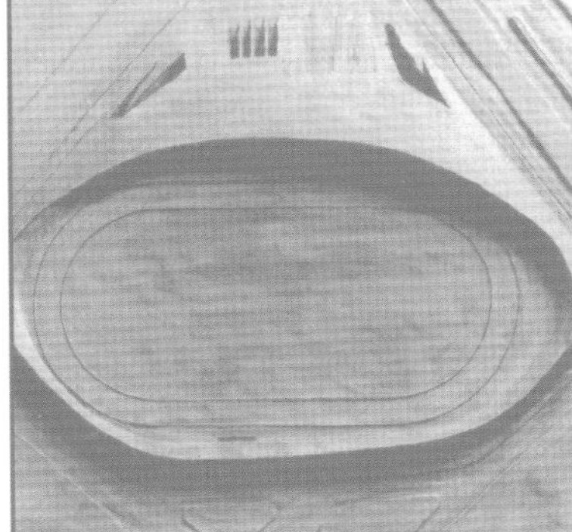

Original text

Ana Rosa de Oliveira
Introduction, Four Horizons, Tower RWE in Essen, Hortus Sanitatis, Hector Petersen Museum, Venice cultural center, Botanical gardens in La Gomera, Rest areas and services, Cultural center Jean Marie Tjibaou in Nouméa, Pompeu Fabra Library in Mataró, Park in Medina del Campo, Alterarions to the Reichstag, Commerzbank in Frankfurt.

Alejandro Bahamón
Santa Cruz de Tenerife Athletic Stadium, "Forest house" Exhibition pavilion, Water purifier in Amiens, House in Lauterach, VPRO head office, Center of overseas archives, Bordeaux-Merignac air-traffic control center, Draguignan house.

Sofia Cheviakof
Barcelona Botanical gardens, Fresh water pavilion, The RVU building, Windpower energy station for expo 2000.

Design and layout

Mireia Casanovas Soley

English translation

Richard-Lewis Rees

Copy editor & proofreader

Julie King

Printed in Spain

Apipe s.l.

LOFT publications
Domènech 9, 2 -2
08012 Barcelona Spain
Tel.: +34 93 218 30 99
Fax: +34 93 237 00 60
loft@loftpublications.com
www.loftpublications.com

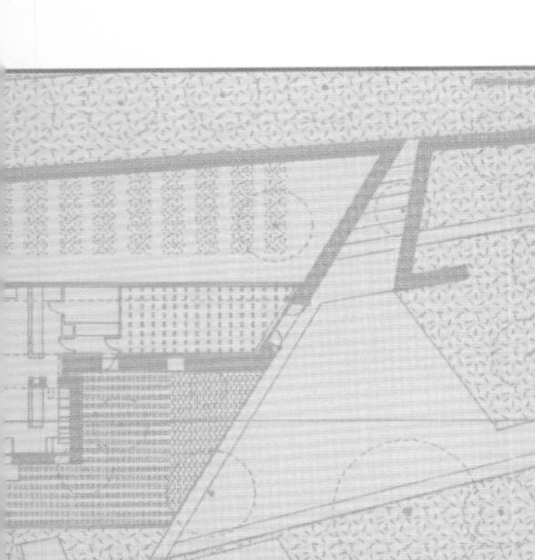

ISBN

84-8185-241-4

Dep. legal

B-36.636/99

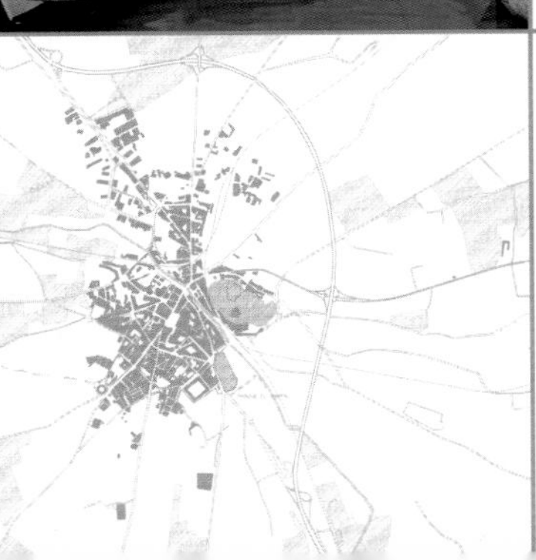

In contemporary architecture, the changes resulting from the introduction of criteria of bioclimatics and sustainability are becoming increasingly important. To speak of sustainability in architecture means conceiving constructions for the future, not only in terms of the physical durability of the building, but also the durability of the planet and its energy resources. In this case, it seems that sustainability would be based on the introduction of a productive model in which available materials and resources are more efficiently used, rather than squandered or ignored. To speak today of the ecology of a building is, in short, to focus on its capacity to integrate environmental and climatic parameters, and to transform them into qualities of space, comfort, and form. Among the strategies of this architecture, it is possible to detect a number of trends, such as optimization of architectural form, orientations and openings; the power of inertia and the exploitation of passive solar energy, and the incorporation of active solar energy (its transformation into heat and electricity), and the application of intelligent systems by which buildings function profitably. Finally, greater emphasis is laid on the use of natural materials, such as wood, which may be reintroduced into the natural cycle. Regarding landscape architecture and the relationship between buildings and their surroundings, the significance of some projects lies in a new link between artifact and nature. Talk is heard of an architecture that, through its interaction with the landscape, establishes a constant negotiation, converting place elements into subjects in their own right. An architecture that exists alongside trees, climate, and topography, and which becomes integrated without mimicry or without causing radical ruptures. Given the deterioration of the environment and the increasing scarcity of resources today, an attitude that neither pillages nor overly protects nature is needed, an attitude that makes rational use of available resources. In short, we must learn to adapt to a new framework capable of imagining and designing what will be required in the future. Some years ago, the advocacy of ecological architecture was somewhat discredited by the very image of this architecture. At the outset, this kind of architecture generally restricted itself to displaying devices of energy saving and ecology rather than integrating them as constituent elements of the project. The result was ugly and more costly buildings. Today, however, sustainable architecture has spread to many places. In Germany, perhaps the country where the idea of ecological construction has taken deepest root, the Reichstag itself has been endowed with a solar dome and a system of natural ventilation. With time, it is believed that the acquisition of ecological awareness, as in Germany, will progress from a simple question of ideology to a real economic factor: 100% ecological buildings, which consume a minimum of energy or generate their own, might one day become an integral part of standard housing programs.

However, it is not yet possible to see clear, unanimous changes taking place. Nonetheless, it is a well-known fact that in processes of socio-educational awareness there are no immediate, spectacular changes, but rather isolated initiatives that gradually come to impregnate people's minds. Bioclimatic architecture is slowly spreading to all levels of society and transforming many areas and viewpoints. And although many projects still restrict the ecological question to one of energy, and only a few conceive ecological construction as a global process (based on urban planning and, besides the orientation of buildings, define form, materials and domotics), they nevertheless point in the right direction, perhaps to change our present and recycle our thinking. Considering that only by optimizing available energy use (moderating expenditure and doing without unnecessary lighting, poor thermal insulation, and so on), we could double its productivity, we can safely say that the most readily available energy source for the immediate future is saving and efficiency, in which case ecological is tantamount to economical. The same discourse must be applied to the cycle of materials. Available literature on architecture that favors ecological questions is still scarce, and is normally restricted to specialists. For this reason, Ecotechture is an attempt to divulge the plurality of ideas concerning the environment by publishing projects developed within ecological parameters.

The book is therefore an approach to different ecological initiatives in architecture as a whole. The works presented provide a global view of ecological construction in terms not only of urban planning but also of landscape architecture, the way buildings are placed in their surroundings, housing, offices, infrastructures, and urban public spaces. The present volume is divided into two sections – From Ecology to Architecture and From Technology to Nature – two trends that appear to oppose one on another but that pursue the same aims: on one hand, the evolution of ecological theory regarding the recycling of materials; the rehabilitation of degraded areas; and the incorporation of natural processes into the project, reflected in specific architectural intentions. And on the other, technological advances resulting from research into the thermal efficiency of buildings, the possibilities of solar energy, and the bioclimatic design of façades. The book's two sections make it possible to include high-tech works (Norman Foster, Renzo Piano, Jourda & Perraudin), projects by architects trained in the landscape discipline (Roche) and, of course, works by experts in the use of recycled or alternative materials (Johnson, Unterrainer, Atengo, Menis & Pastrana). The book features both projects at the design stage and completed works. Ecotechture presents both architecture in which professionals apply high-tech solutions and increasingly sophisticated domotic systems, and ecological experiments conducted with less technology and lower costs, although they are equally telling. Different strategies have generated initiatives that cannot entirely "do without" the site (as in the case of landscape architecture), and architectures conceived as "another" nature, built as a topography for a specific place. The book also deals with ecology in the domestic sphere, which through more modest means, such as compact panels, uses passive solar energy, wood for construction and exterior cladding, and roof gardens. In these cases, the human factor is associated with changes in attitude. Inhabitants are instilled with sensitivity and responsibility, and ecology becomes democratized. Our objective is present an increasingly important theme, bearing in mind the fact that if environmental problems exist, it is not because ecological mechanisms have suddenly broken down (there are no ecologically generated problems as such), but because relations between our species and the environment have entered a critical phase. At a time in which environmental problems require imagination with which to develop new economic and development paradigms, we feel it is necessary to divulge those initiatives that propose new environmental concepts that integrate ethical, aesthetic, and technological dimensions. The presentation of these projects also constitutes a challenge: by publishing them, we set out to show that ecological architecture must not remain restricted to a privileged few but become available to everyone and established as a norm. Behind ecology, there is a social phenomenon: people have access to technology and ecological materials thanks to active individual participation in the conception, construction, and preservation of buildings.

From ecology to architecture

architecture as topography

architecture as topography
architecture as topography
architecture as topography
architecture as topography
architecture as topography
architecture as topography

architecture as topography

architecture as topography

architecture as topography

VPRO Head office

MVRDV

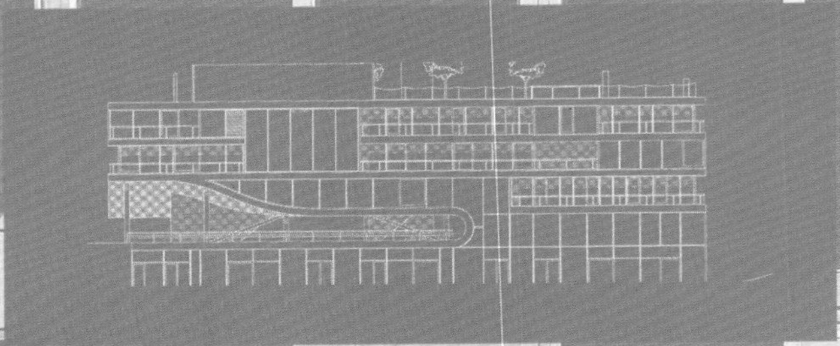

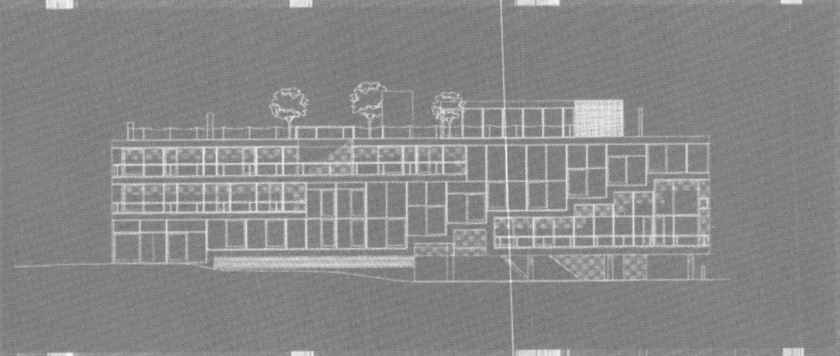

Location: Hilversum, Holland

Client: VPRO, Hilversum

Construction date: 1997

Architects: MVRDV

Collaborators: Stefan Witteman, Alex Brouwer, Joost Glissenaar

Photographs: Christian Richters

SG-51-VT
NV-RT-34
gti
NL

Maximum Impact from a Minimal Space

One of the dilemmas facing contemporary architecture is how to solve the problem of building while conserving the landscape. In ecological terms, land development is perhaps the main cause of deterioration of the natural environment. And in certain places, such as Holland, where available land is scarce and consequently very expensive, concern with this problem is even greater. The challenge therefore lies in how to create architectural models that generate the maximum variety of types and recreate certain traditional environments in a minimal space. Compactness, which characterizes this project for the head office of the VPRO audiovisual company, is therefore a fundamental factor when it comes to establishing a harmonious dialogue between architecture and landscape.

For many years, this company was divided among 13 locales scattered throughout the city, a situation that played a vital role in the creation of VPRO's identity. The staff members, accustomed to working in apartment rooms, attics, or first-floor venues, were now required to find their niche in a "real" ofice environment. When it came to designing the new headquarters, the burning question was whether the informal atmosphere of the old offices, which had an important influence on the programs produced there, could find its place in a modern office complex designed according to principles of maximum efficiency. In other words, could "informality" survive an increase in scale?

Given the national urban planning restrictions on zoning and maximum height, compactness led to the creation of "Holland's deepest office block." The vegetation that formerly occupied the site where the building now stands was replaced by a roof-lawn, beneath which a "geological form" defines the building's different levels. These levels are connected by a variety of spatial strategies such as ramps, sloping floors, monumental stairs, and small ascents, all of which mark out an itinerary towards the roof. A "precise bombardment" produced a winding series of patios that allow natural light to penetrate and provide views of the surrounding landscape. The result is an open-plan office where the relationship between interior and exterior is established in a diaphanous way.

Differences of height in the resulting interior space, in combination with the wings generated by the voids, produce a wide range of work environments to accommodate the ever-changing demands of VPRO business. The rooms, attic, hall, patio and terrace all echo the company's former premises. The variety of spaces is reflected in the front façade, which uses 35 different types of glass to create a "data landscape." Colors, reflective quality, and degree of transparency were determining factors when it came to placing the glass. In this sense, the interior's spatial quality is reflected in a kind of "rose window." The plaques are supported by a mesh of columns and stable supports that, in combination with the completely open façade, guarantee maximum transparency for the interior spaces.

The way the building has been constructed evokes old villas: the ceilings are genuine and the walls, instead of prefabricated, are made of stone, metal, timber or plastic. There are no fitted carpets, only Persian and sisal rugs. Neither are there small windows, but rather sliding glass panels one floor in height that provide most of the rooms with access to a garden, balcony, terrace or patio. Terms such as compactness, spatial differentiation, and links with the surrounding landscape best define this project, which strategically exploits a minimal area of building land and manages to meet the demands of a flexible program while affecting the natural environment as little as possible.

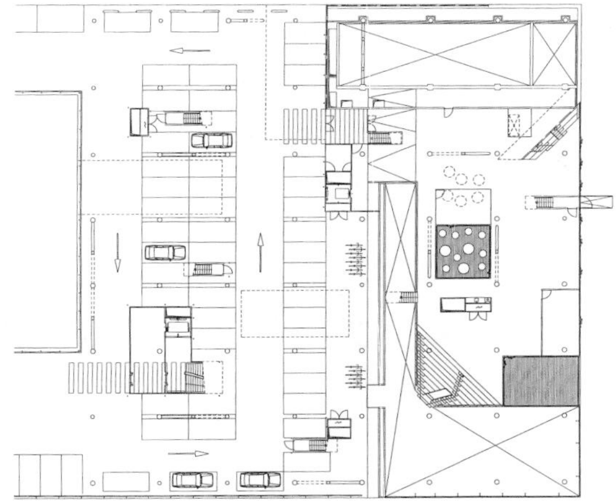

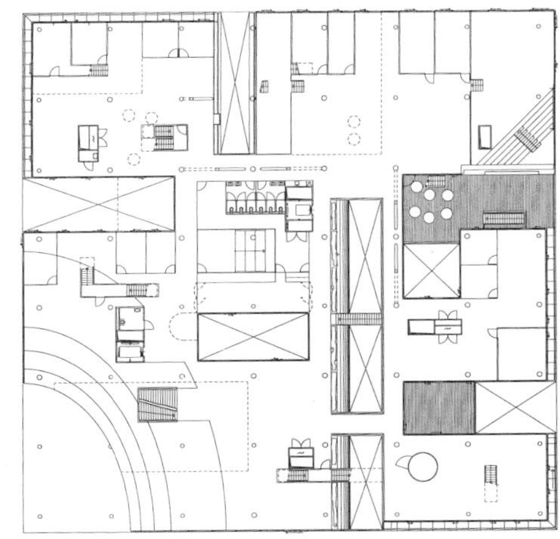

The block is characterized by compactness, in accordance with existing urban building regulations, which limited maximum height. The block was endowed with considerable depth and the surfaces fully exploited by reducing the number of corridors

The frontiers between interior and exterior are blurred on an open-plan floor. The existing vegetation was replaced by a roof garden

The complex functional program required by the clients was fulfilled with a wide variety of environments. The different heights of the interior spaces and voids brings diversity to the building

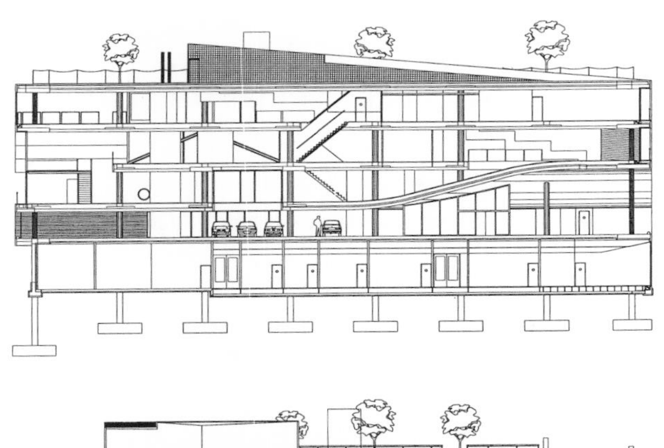

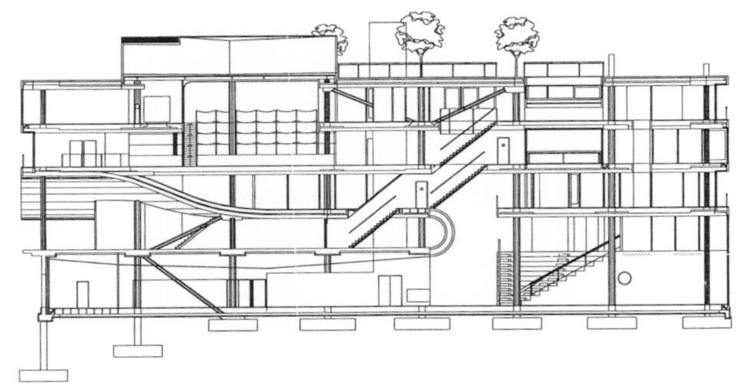

The RVU Building

MVRDV

Location: **Hilversum, Holland**

Client: **RVU Hilversum**

Construction date: **1997**

Architects: **MVRDV**

Collaborators: **Willem Timmer, Duzan Doepel, Eline Strijkers**

Photographs: **Christian Richters**

The Volume that Arises from the Earth

The RVU is one of the buildings that forms the "campus" of the VPRO, VARA, NPS, and RVU television chains in Hilversum, Holland. In order to establish an ecological link with the adjacent Media Park, the essential idea was to create the impression of a site on which nothing had been built.

Both the façades and the roof of the raised part are clad with corten steel, a relatively new material that has a rusty appearance. The RVU Building is split lengthwise into two halves by the staircase, which emerges onto the roof to define a pedestrian path. Part of the street cuts through the building along the whole of its length and ends at the lowest level of the campus. Access to the building is gained at its very core, on one of the stair landings.

The interior consists of an office area divided into three zones, each with its own administrative characteristics in order to better accommodate the company's different departments: a zone with offices arranged randomly; a zone with a double corridor flanked by individual offices; and a third zone with a central catwalk. The cafeteria is situated on the suspended part. Here, the space is cut by a glass partition through which it is possible to contemplate a panoramic view of the landscape and campus. Beneath this point, where the building juts out from the slope, a porch emerges as a disembarkation point for visitors that includes the air-conditioning units and a bicycle park. Its flooring consists of fragments of lava interspersed with floodlights that illuminate the roof like live coals.

The building seems to sprout from the ground, as if it were a part of the earth, or as if the topography had decided to unearth it and reveal the glazed front façade as a wound, a cut, or an interruption.

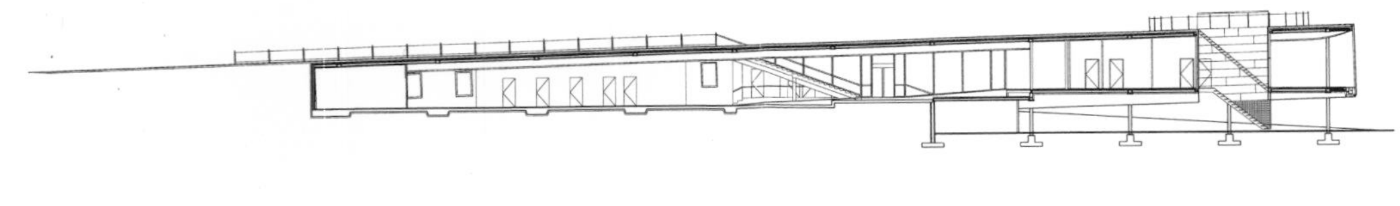

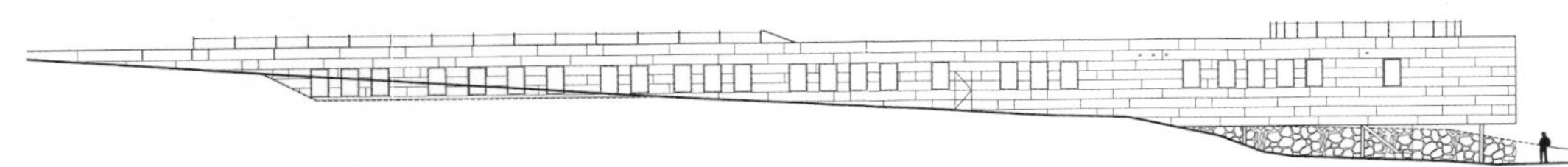

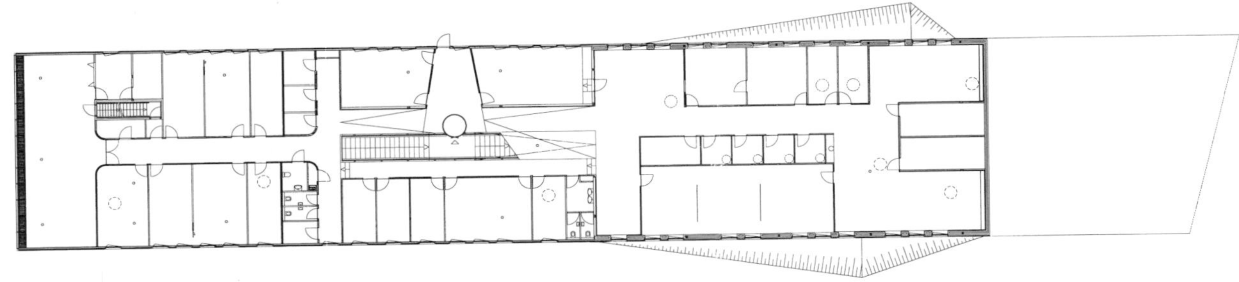

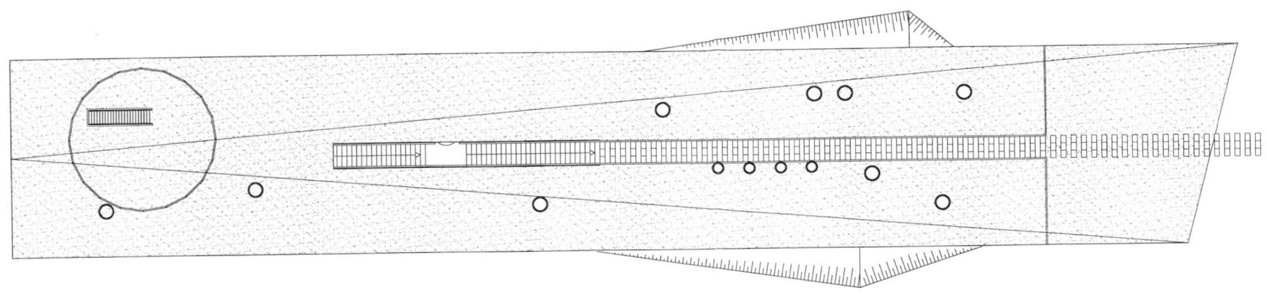

The building is subtly inserted into the landscape, and its roof garden acts as a belvedere from which to contemplate the adjacent park.

The interior includes a continuous work area divided into three zones, each of which contains different parts of the functional program. Each zone is typologically differentiated from the rest

fresh water pavilion

NOX Architects

Location: **Neelte Jans, Netherlands**

Client: **Water Management Ministry**

Construction Date: **1997**

Architects: **NOX Architects**

A Complete Fusion of Body, Environment, and Technology

This pavilion in Zeeland, Holland is a turbulent combination of fragile and resilient, human flesh, concrete, and metal, and interactive electronics and water. A complete fusion of body, environment, and technology, the design is based on the combination of computer science and architecture.

H_2O eXPO is an "exhibit/artifact" dedicated to water. Two pavilions make up the exhibit, the Salt Water Pavilion designed by Kas Oosterhuis and the interconnected Fresh Water Structure..

The fresh water part, designed by NOX, is both a building and an exhibition, where geometry, architecture, and installation combine to form a structure that does not 'contain' an exhibition, in the classical sense of a museum. Instead, the images and sounds that emerge depend on the visitor's activities. The visitors have to become part of the water to go through the building. The interactivity, the in-between-ness of subject and environment, of object and event, begins with geometry.

The building's shape is accomplished by warping 14 ellipses, sixty-five meters long, in a flowing manner. Inside the building, walking is like falling; the floors are not horizontal, and there is no reference to the horizon.

This "deformation" of the building relates directly to the constant mutation of the created environment, which responds to visitors in an interactive manner, through sensors that monitor their movements.

The first part of the building starts with a three-dimensional door and is constantly flooded with water in different ways. Upon entering there is the "glacier-tunnel," a completely frozen space with melting water spilling over the floor. Then there are "springs" spraying mist and water, the "rain bowl" with strobe lit rain that spurts up from a bowl, and the "well." The well contains 120,000 liters of water and has its own program of projections and light. It also throws everything else off balance. It becomes another type of horizon, an interior one, that is vertical, not horizontal, and works as an axis for vertigo, for falling.

There are different kinds of sensors that detect the presence of visitors and, by way of a system of multiple combinations, induce changes in the building. Some sensors are connected to a laser beam projecting a grid that converts the visitor's every motion into movements of virtual water. Every time someone walks through a beam of infrared light, a wave goes through the projected grid.

Other sensors are connected to a system of blue lamps running along the building's ceiling. When they are activated, a wave of blue light sweeps through the whole interior and accelerates like a reactivated heartbeat. With four different types of controls, the visitors can create any type of interference on these waves. There is also a projected sphere that can change shape like a water droplet at zero gravity.

The sound system works in combination with the light and real-time projections. All sensors are connected to CD-ROMs with sound-samplers that can be deformed, bent, and stretched. The sound itself can also change places. For instance, it can be electronically pulled out of the well, or pulled towards the string of light, which is also the main support for the sound system. All of this adds to the feeling of movement and activity inherent to the building.

We speak of "liquid architecture" when a structure generates geometry of flow and turbulence and dissolves everything solid and crystalline, not only the materials, but also the function and program. By fusing floor and wall, floor and screen, surface and interface, a plastic, liquid, and haptic architecture is achieved. It synthesizes action and vision within a single experiment.

This piece is conceived to demonstrate—through its architecture and the use of different interactive multimedia systems—one of the vital elements in nature, the environment, and humankind: water.

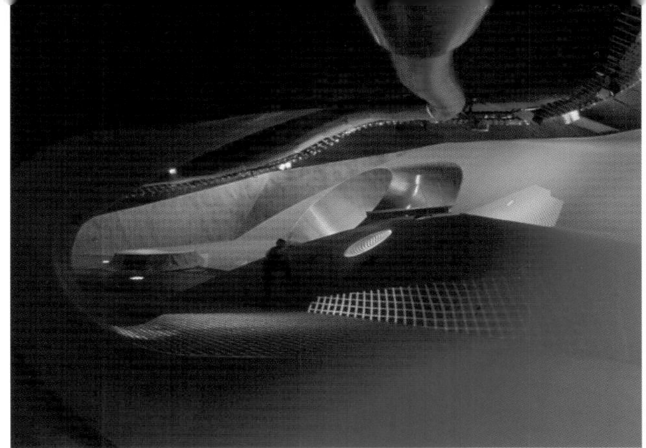

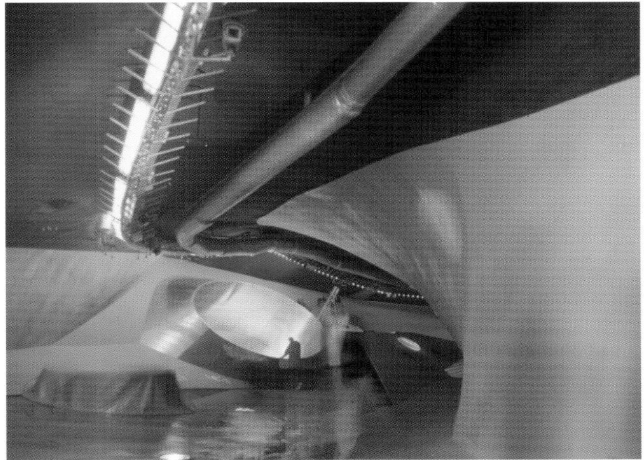

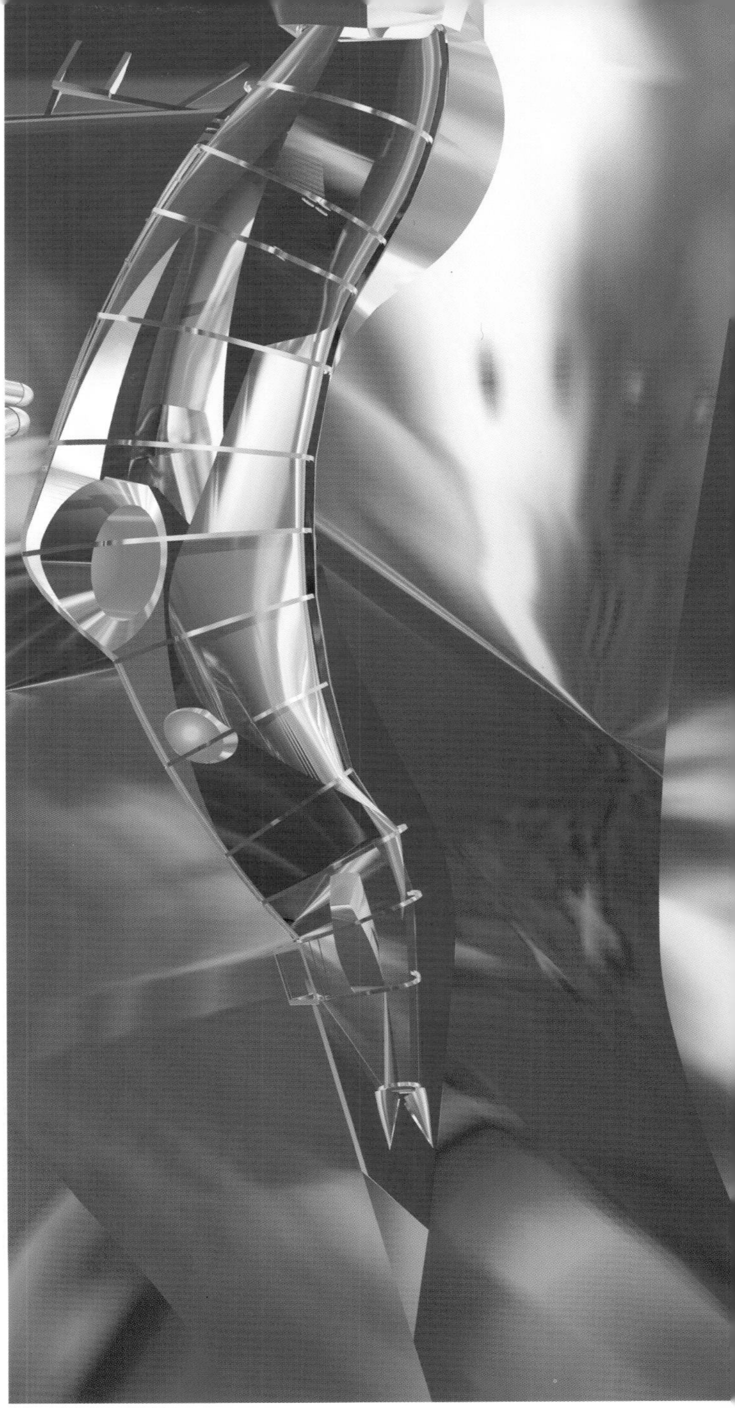

The Pavilion is a building/exhibition unit which integrates geometry, architecture and installation. Instead of containing the exhibition in the classic sense, it presents and changes it according to the itinerary and actions of the visitor. It incorporates advanced software systems that detect the movement of the audience and present a variety of reactions

rest areas and services

Jensen + Skodvin

Location: **Norway**

Client: **Department of Tourism**

Construction Date: **1997**

Architects: **Jensen + Skodvin**

Photography: **Jensen + Skodvin**

Elements in the Landscape that Bring us Closer to Nature

The Norwegian Tourism Program was established to increase the choice of road services for travelers along the most popular tourist routes. With this premise, the program sponsored a competition in 1995 for the design of rest areas, equipment, and services for the roads of the Oppland y Sogn og Fjordane districts. Of the four design teams chosen, only the project executed by Jensen & Skodvin is presented here.

The projects involve an extensive program that includes the development of the rest areas themselves, parking, and new elements like information systems, parapets, signage, and furniture.

The assignment consisted of sixteen rest areas and services for two tourist routes in the northeast of Norway. The roads link Lom, Gaupne, Grotti, and Oppstryn and border some of the country´s most representative landscapes, such as the Stryhejellsvegen massif with some of Norway's tallest mountains. There are two levels of intervention: first, planning and management of the existing resources, views, topography, and floors—all directly related to the design of the rest areas, and secondly, the detailing of equipment and furniture. The shape of benches, tables, facilities, information panels, fences, walkways, and tree guards is defined more by their function than by their placement. A sort of catalogue of elements is established as a whole, so that mass production is available for any size order. Subsequently, detail design work on each rest area adjusts the pieces to their specific location. The new elements are placed with a view to protect, inform, and assist the traveler, or simply to clarify and highlight surrounding scenery.

Thus, the distribution of equipment, the sheltering walls against the glacial winds, the walkways leading to the mountains, and so on, draw a boundary between an "untouchable Nature" and the Nature delicately transformed by man. This tampering is subtle in its formulation, despite the strict geometry of the furniture. It feels adequate—because of the scale and the resolute landscape—to opt for simplification and versatility in the parts and to give priority to the relationships they establish among themselves and with their immediate surroundings. In this sense, the structure becomes a sort of landmark for the traveler to proceed through the region feeling supported, to enjoy the experience of confronting a primordial force and to ponder the strange absence of human presence in the landscape. The project presents different ways of stepping into the Norwegian landscape; planning the different elements starts with their function and culminates in their placement on the site. This is applied to the shaping of benches, facilities, information panels, and viewpoints. The power of the landscape calls for strong geometric forms. Jensen + Skovdin have opted for simple and versatile furniture, subtle additions to an overwhelming landscape.

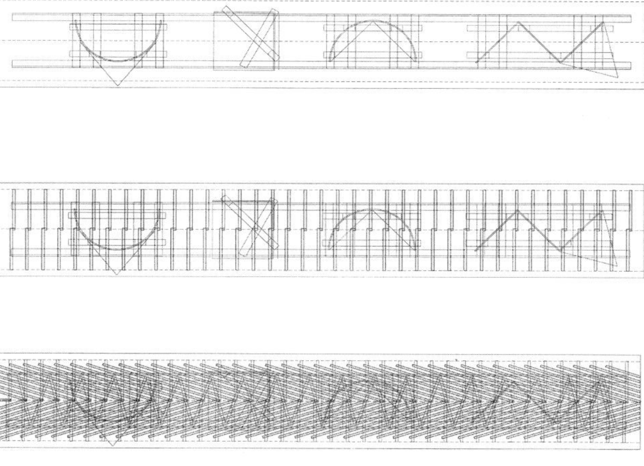

The project consists of different interventions on the Norwegian landscape.
The design of the different elements takes into account functionality and is detailed with the presence of artifacts on the site. This order determines the shape of the benches, information points and services

The strength of the landscape requires acute geometrical shapes. Jensen + Skovdin selected simple, versatile furniture which complements the stunning enviroment

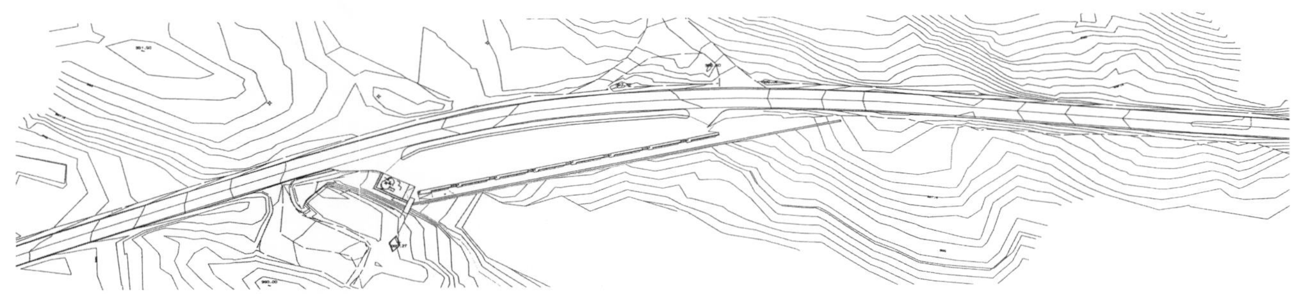

Landscape alterations

Landscape alterat

Landscape alterations

Landscape alterations

Landscape alterations

scape alterations

Landscape alterations

Landscape alterati

ndscape alterations

Landscape alterations

Landscape altera

Landscape alterations

Landscape alterations

Landscape alteratior

scape alterations

Landscape alterations

Landscape altera

Landsc

andscape alterations

Lansdcape alterations

Landscape

ndscape laterations

Landscape alterati

Landscape alterations

ons

dscape alterations

ns

ons

Landscape alterations

andscape alterations

ns

alterations

terations

Botanical Gardens in La Gomera

Artengo, Menis & Pastrana Architects

Location: La Gomera, Spain

Client: Excmo. Cabildo de La Gomera

Construction date: 1998

Architects: Artengo Menis and Pastrana

Collaborators: David Branwell

Photography: Jordi Bernadó and AMP Arquitectos

The Potential of the Land for Human Knowledge

The Discovery Botanical Gardens are located in Vallehermoso, at the north side of La Gomera, one of the Canary Islands. They are conceived as a center for living documentation, in an attempt to reflect the island's leading role as a maritime link for the Discovery routes and as a platform for cultural exchange between Europe and the Americas. Vegetation illustrates this cultural interaction. In one way or another, all the species collected for the gardens were involved in the fruitful plant exchange that took place between the continents.

Thanks to its atmospheric, orographic and pedologic conditions, the selected site is the ideal environment for the cultivation of a great variety of species, from mild to tropical.

Two broad areas structure the Botanical Gardens and comply with traditional flora classification. On one of the stretches, vegetation is grouped by criteria such as medicinal and practical use, and succulent, greenhouse, hothouse, and palms. The other stretch groups vegetation by geographic region: Gomerian, Macaronesian, European introduced in America, and American introduced in Europe. The geographic section occupies the garden's main area and is considered its core. The species are assembled according to their origin and habitat, avoiding rigid arrangements like rows. The plants define the character of the trails and sitting areas, where their most relevant characteristics are carefully enhanced.

The leading principle–and what has become the true essence of the project–was utmost respect for the preexisting conditions of the place and its legacy. Initially, it was important to clarify the spatial relations already in place.

Centenarian palm trees were salvaged and the site configuration was respected by terracing the garden patches. Only a few terraces were slanted differently, in a garden that falls towards a gully. A grid of trails, with smoothly zigzagging ramps, was superimposed over this preexisting configuration, which is regulated and irrigated gently. A stone wall envelops the premises and, at one point, becomes part of the nursery by blending into the local typology.

The materials used are primitive in order to infuse the work with a timeless character. The stone for the garden's walls, paths, ramps, and stairs is finished with bastardized mortar to allow liquens and rupicola plants to root with time. The interior pedestrian spaces are treated with pulverized clay topped with compacted gravel.

An information and service center is set like a "hanging rock" over the Botanical Gardens. This building is a stair-stepped costruction leaning against the terrain's rocky slope and appears to be intended by the mountain, as if it were continuing its stratification over the garden. It is a transitory space, where visitors are welcomed and informed before starting their visit.

The architectural premise is similar to the treatment of the landscape. In both cases, preexisting conditions are to be brought up to date. The project considers the tensions of the place and strives to create a dialogue with the terrain. Architects carefully studied the site in order to make the most of the setting. They were receptive to the land and its natural forms and colonization styles. The outcome is a building meant for human use which brings the guests and nature closer to one another.

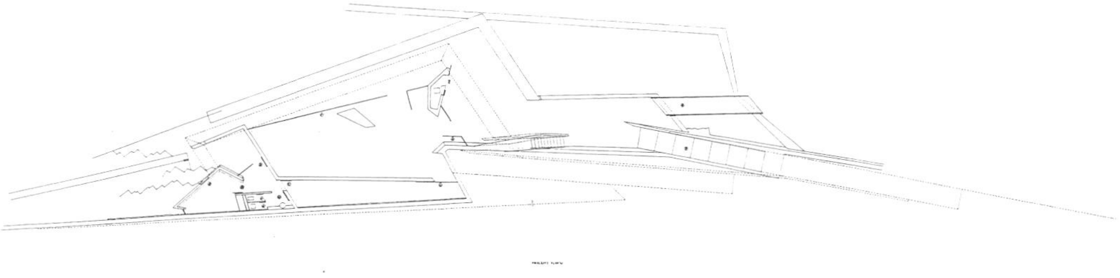

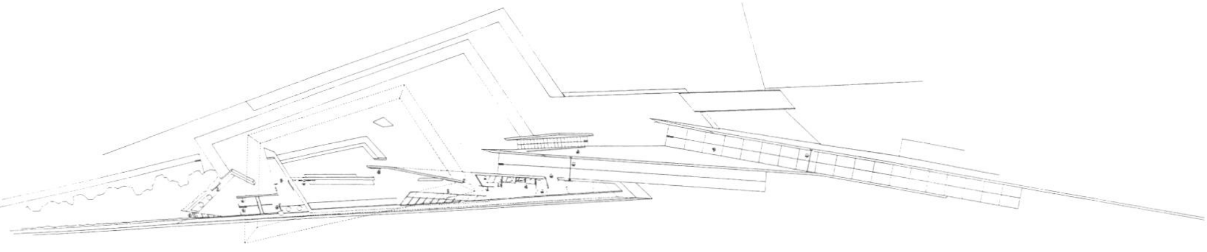

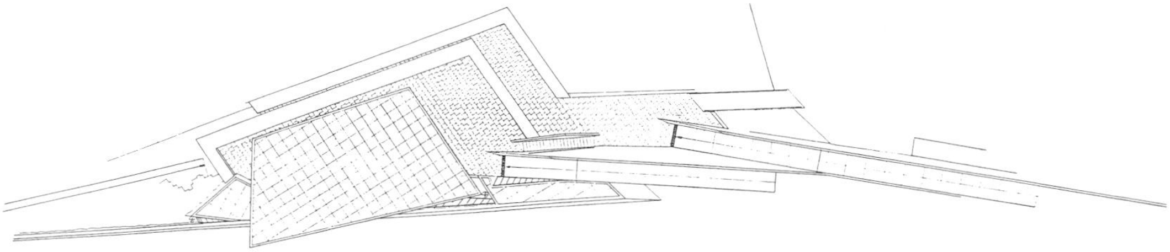

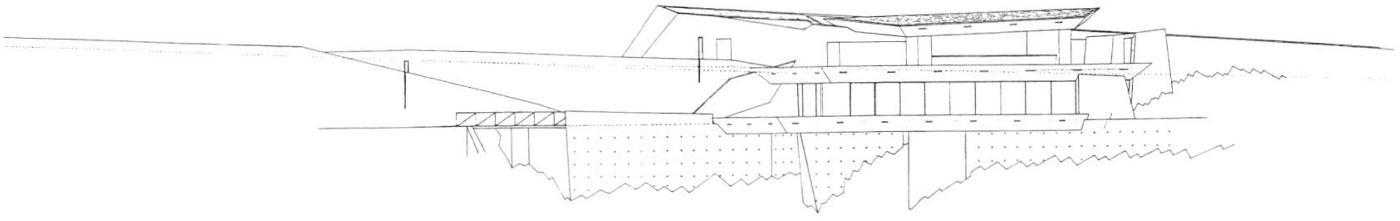

The project's main objective for the project was to provide the local residents with a tranquil and gentle garden environment and center for live documentation that would reflect the significant role of the island as a platform for cultural exchange.

The existing terrain was composed of cultivated fields by the edge of a gully. The land keeps its configuration; only a few terraces change grade so that the garden slopes into the ravine

The gardens are conceived as a compact unit, using a few basic fabrics and primitive construction elements, which infuse the work with a timeless character

Landscaping of the A85 freeway

Bernard Lassus et Associés

Location: **A85 freeway, Angers-Tours-Vierzon, France**

Client: **Société Cofiroute**

Construction date: **1997**

Architects: **Bernard Lassus et Associés**

Solution to the Highway's Effect on the Landscape

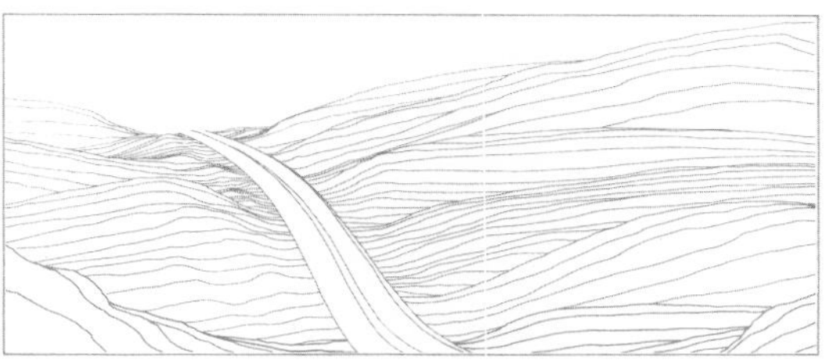

Bernard Lassus' design embraces all aspects relative to the impact of a new section of freeway on countryside which is particularly attractive. His design criteria was based on the search for fresh and alternative solutions to the usual system of mechanically wrought cuttings and embankments which cleave through the countryside and sever the visual nexus between the driver and the surrounding landscape. So often a new highway appears as an unwelcome intrusion into the lives of the local inhabitants.

Lassus' design takes into account the visual point of view of both the driver and the local inhabitants and looks for ways in which both groups can experience a relationship with the resulting landscape. To this end, he proposed solutions for two main areas: the system of cuttings and embankments, and the construction of rest areas, specifically the service area that adjoins the Étang de Ténières, a new artificial lake created for the project. He also devised a strategy for the new vegetation and plantings.

In his approach to the necessary cuttings and embankments, Lassus seeks an alternative to the well-used weapon of simply cleaving through the existing topography to make way for the new road. His innovative approach offers a meticulous study which envisages the new topographical order in three dimensions, so that the transition between the new planes generated by the construction and the surrounding landscape should have as much continuity as possible. At the points where the freeway follows a different gradient from that of the surrounding topography, Lassus proposes a series of interrupted cuttings that allow the driver to see the surrounding countryside at certain points. At other points, such as the Corzé interchange, the architect uses a new three-dimensional strategy of slopes and embankments so that the landscape, the elongated strand of freeway and the system of planes which unite them are as continuous as possible.

The strategy of modifying the existing topography is accompanied by a parallel strategy carried out on the vegetation and the new plantations of trees. At some points, Lassus has established copses of trees, which run perpendicular to the road, again permitting glimpses of the far horizon and ensuring that this new element does not cut off the view. At other points on the long, straight stretches of freeway, Lassus plants trees parallel to the road, but set back from it. The vegetation seems to carve out a channel with the freeway at its center. Fields occupy the space between the trees and the road, and where these slope, they do so smoothly and gently. In the end, the fields and the vegetation become the principal components of Lassus' design and the dry, featureless, truncated embankments so often seen on freeways disappear. Eliminating this screen means that the drivers and the local inhabitants experience the same view of the vegetation and fields.

Pursuing the same ideal of connecting the freeway with the land, the architect built a rest area around an artificial lake. A bridge between the experience of driving and that of being in the country, the Étang des Ténières rest area has the lake as its center, where it is possible to use the small boats provided or even to swim from the artificial beaches. The main leisure element of the area is the water itself, a natural element which integrates easily into the landscape.

The importance of Lassus' design is that it can be typified and extrapolated to other circumstances, since it addresses a problem which is omnipresent in our modern-day society: the integration of major highways into the landscape. This design seeks to resolve the problem or at least to tone it down.

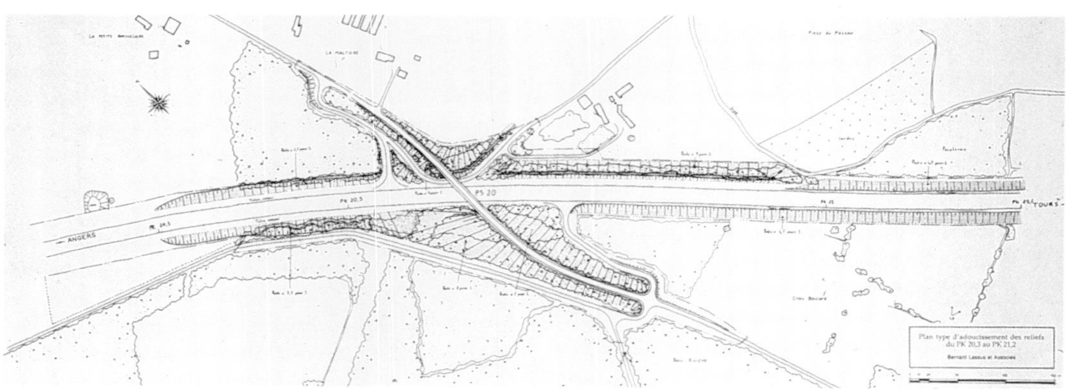
ANGERS
TOURS
PS 20
Plan type d'adoucissement des reliefs
du PK 20,3 au PK 21,2
Bernard Lassus et Associés

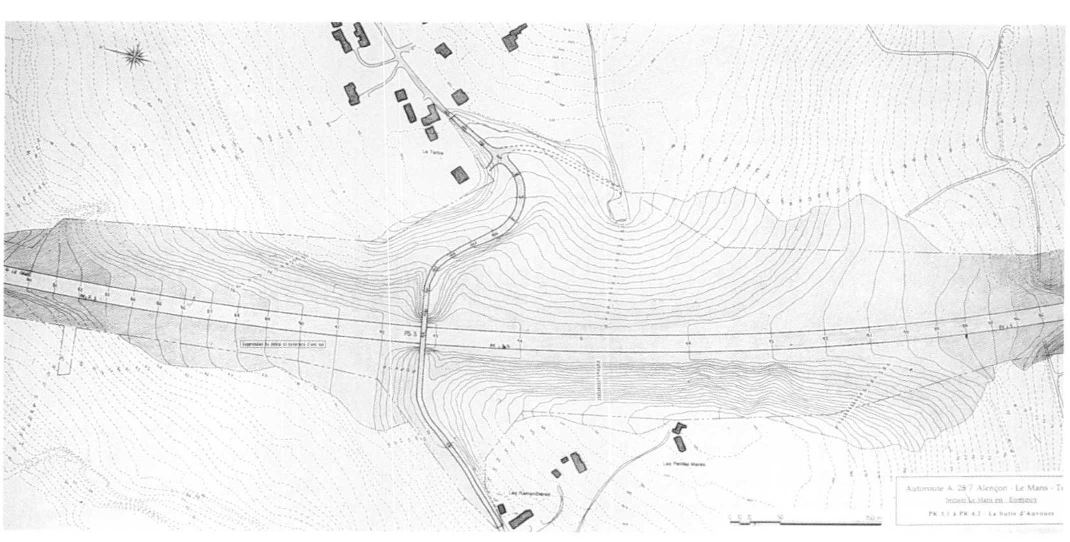
PS 3
Autoroute A. 28 7 Alençon - Le Mans - T
PK 3,1 à PK 4,2 : La butte d'Auvours

In some cases, the new plantations of trees are placed perpendicular to the road, which provides drivers with a vision of the horizon and thus an overall perception of the countryside around them

santa cruz de Tenerife athletic stadium

Artengo, Menis & Pastrana

Location: Santa Cruz de Tenerife, Spain

Architects: Artengo, Menis & Pastrana

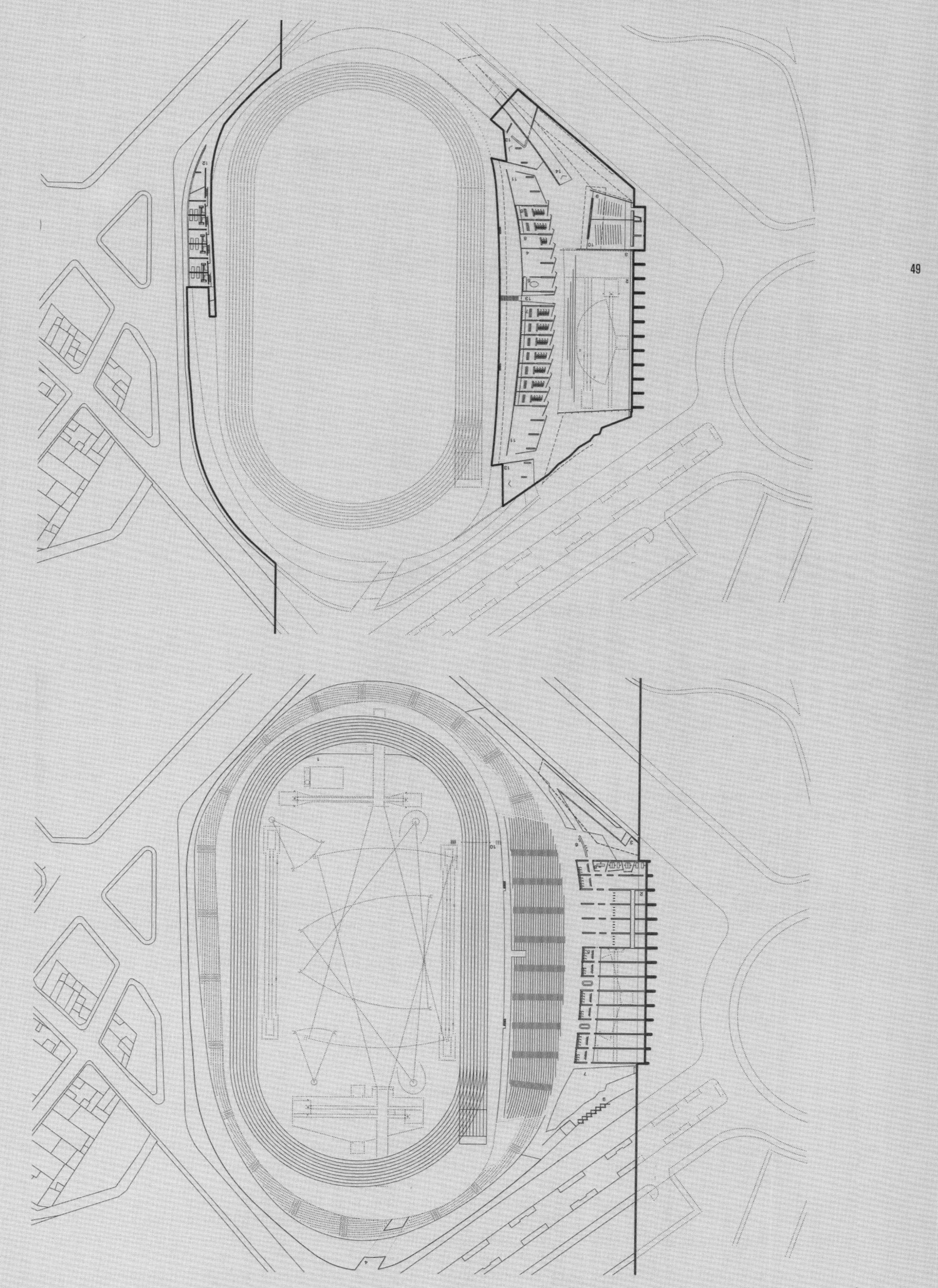

Infrastructure and Public Life

Urban models are defined, more and more, by the dissolution of boundaries between city and territory. Infrastructures, road systems, and large buildings that attempt to belong to a regional, or even universal, scale shape the urban structure. Now that awareness of the environmental impact of such structures has shifted to the forefront, these infrastructures tend to relate to both the traditional city around them and the natural terrain below. The main challenge of the Santa Cruz de Tenerife Athletic Stadium commission is achieving integration within the urban fabric and the natural landscape, despite the object's monumental nature of the object. In a way, the project is about establishing a new ecological vision for large-scale interventions.

The sports facility approaches the site from the front, making use of the slightly inclined topography. The stands extend over a continuous peripheral slope that envelops and protects the athletic field. The result is an embankment on one side and an excavation on the other. The two balance each other and minimize cutting of the land.

On the street level of the embankment, at the top of the site, access to the sport facilities is through a public square that is extended as a cover over the stands. A pathway of ramps to one side takes the athletes to the High Performance Center, where they have direct access to the field. Four large openings in the square provide access for the audience. Various slits and apertures belong to a system of interior lighting and ventilation. As a whole, the result is an access area that subtly blends into the surrounding urban fabric. A peripheral incline of the terrain, resulting from the land moved during excavation, completes the program required for the stands and results in a compact and uniform proposal.

The volumes are practically camouflaged into the background by planting the object into the setting. This is a huge architectonic element, planned for 6,000 spectators, which supports a public area and a vast square. If is inside the city but meant on a regional scale. In a program where structural components have great relevance, the construction system is carefully planned in order to establish the same standards for economical efficiency and low environmental impact. It is proposed as a repetitive scheme of concrete panels, which also facilitate understanding of the work and short-term execution. Likewise, the architects selected high-resistance materials for the interior and exterior lining in anticipation rough and intense public use of the facilities, with minimum maintenance.

However, the most surprising aspect of this concrete superstructure is its passive solar system design. Ventilation and lighting for the High Performance Center and the administrative quarters are achieved naturally by th light wells and crown systems established in the access square. To enhance ventilation on the inside, and even at the stands, the roofing is built like a solar collector to the scale of the facility. The metallic material used reaches high temperatures allowing air circulation though its double siding, like a giant chimney, with an air renovation every thirty minutes. This gigantic eaves is oriented southeast, in order to protect the section of the stands receiving more sun.

We are at a place and time where infrastructures define the landscape; how they compare to the natural surroundings and how they relate to the cities has tremendous weight. Some areas overcome their lack of identity by becoming fundamental points of interaction between man, city, and environment. Now, the city opens to the terrain and becomes part of the landscape.

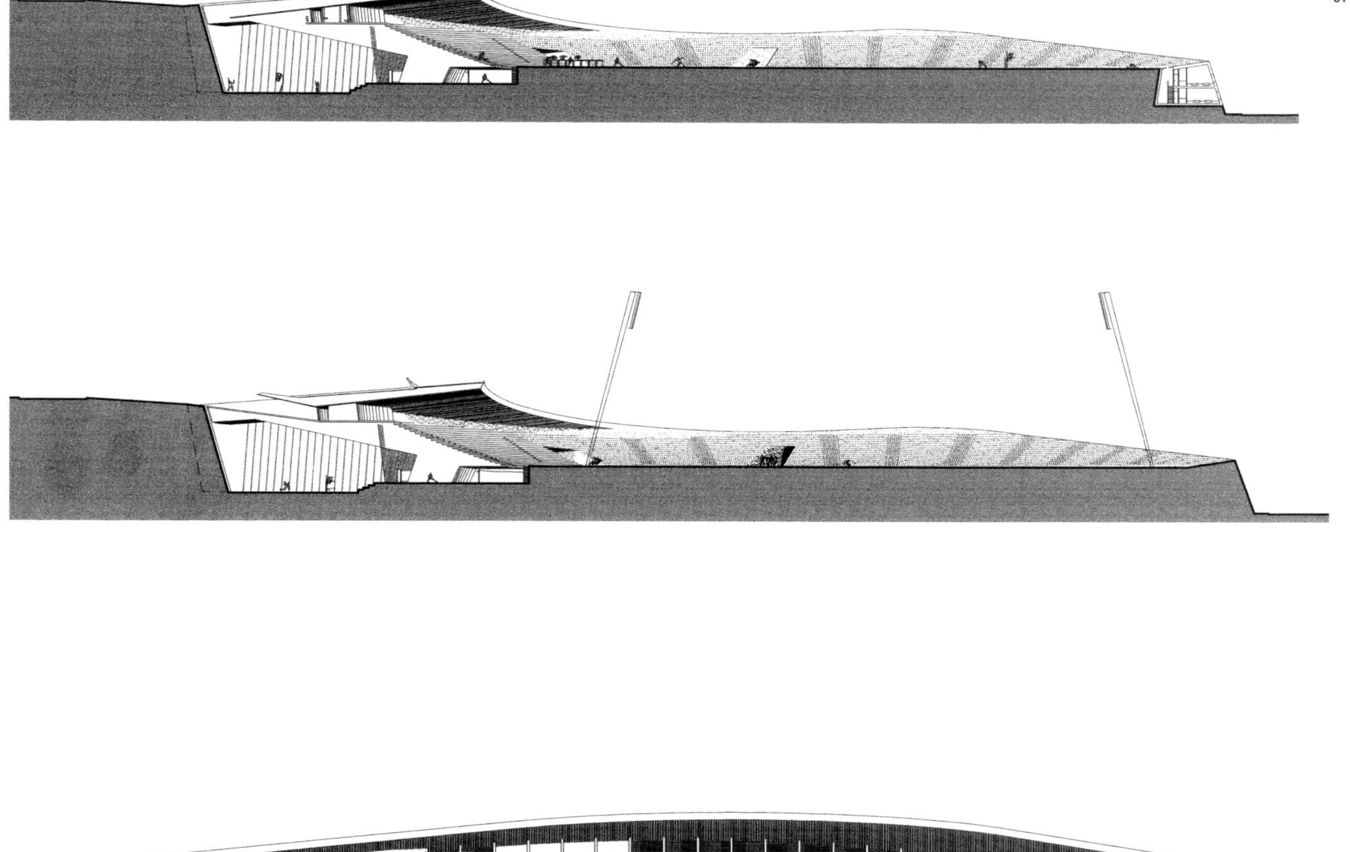

Taking advantage of the sloping topography of the site, the stadium's large horizontal platform is placed on a halfway level permitting landscaped banks to act as stands. A compact and uniform image for the facilities is achieved.

park in Medina del campo

Jubert - Santacana Arquitectes

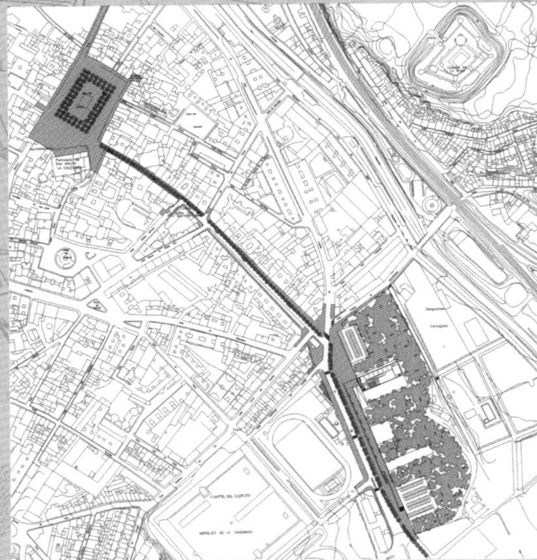

Location: **Medina del Campo, Spain**

Client: **City Hall of Medina del Campo**

Architects: **Jubert-Santacana Arquitectes**

Collaborators: **Teresa Galí, Elisabeth Fauria, Julia Galí, Pedro Cavaller**

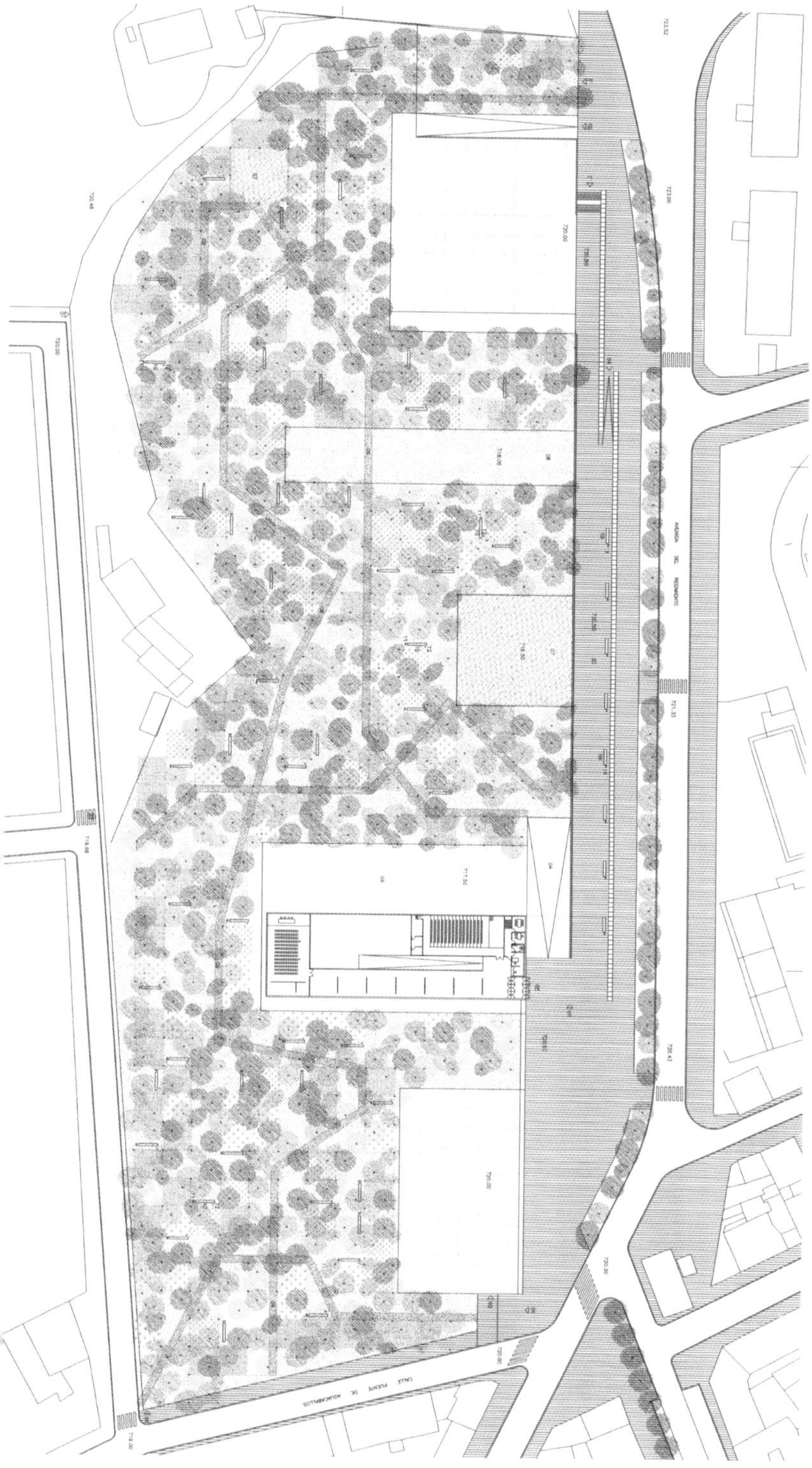

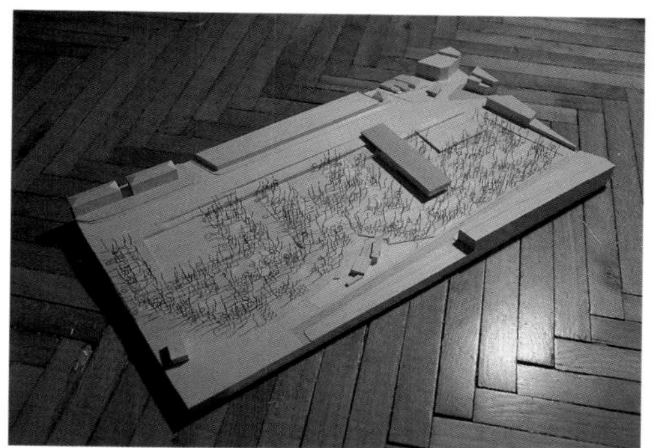

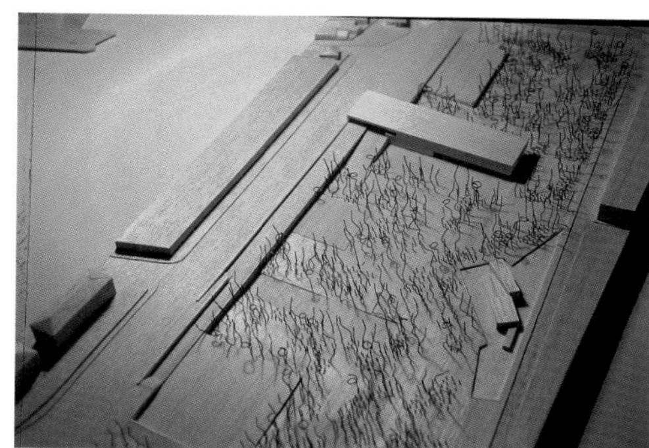

A Park To Be Enjoyed

This project won the competition for a new public park in the area known as "El Chopal," in the southern part of the urban nucleus of Medina del Campo. In addition to the park, the brief included the construction of a multi-purpose building of up to 30,000 square feet and a parking lot for 150-200 vehicles.

The thoroughfares that delimit the site and the surrounding buildings made it difficult to upgrade the area. However, this project by Lluís Jubert and Eugènia Santacana achieved a simple yet forceful intervention in the landscape. The final result is a leisure zone for the local population that includes a magnificent park, formerly a poplar grove, and a field of wild vegetation.

The architects enlarged and changed the section of the existing promenade, splitting it into two walkways at different levels above the park. By establishing links with the city and giving rise to the park's structure, the walkways acted as a catalyst for the rest of the interventions.

The promenade is connected to the city center by the street leading to the Plaza Mayor. Elements constructed at a lower level back onto it and form platforms above the park. The idea was to create two differentiated structures. One is an enclosed constructed system comprising the promenade-belvedere over the park from which the buildings and parking lot are "suspended." The other is a structure that creates a "forest-garden" by combining leafy trees and shrubs.

This dual structure provides great flexibility, creating a bower where people may stroll and relax, protected from the city. The built area containing the services and dependencies is independent from the park itself.

The parking lot consists of two different zones: one in the part that connects with the entry to the city, which is linked to the lower of the two promenades and stretches up to the building's entrance; and the other is located at the opposite end, slightly below the access level to the building.

The building is highly restrained and acts as a subtle transition element between the promenade and the park below, a link between the park's interior and exterior spaces. Access to the building is gained from the promenade, through a porch that is the park's main entrance. The floor above contains the classrooms, auditorium, conference room and a ramp that leads down to the floor below. On this lower level, there is a large, multi-purpose space related both visually and physically to the park.

The lower part of the site contains the park itself. Deciduous trees were strategically planted to create a wide variety of situations in time and space by playing with growth rates, density of plantation and the periods of flowering and leaf fall. The species were selected according to how their characteristics relate to the area: kind of soil, irrigation needs, growth rate, and so on.

An interesting aspect of the project is the creation of 535 square-foot modules, each one containing five trees of different species and size, and shrubs with different heights. The combinaion of modules and the variation of the tree species they contain made it possible in a project of this scale to plant the entire zone without having to conceive it on a plant-by-plant basis.

The forest mass also contains clearings covered with lawns, and fine sand and stones, which define the zones of intensive use. The paths marked out with stones are arranged on homogeneous paving. The define the itineraries and the layout of the park furniture.

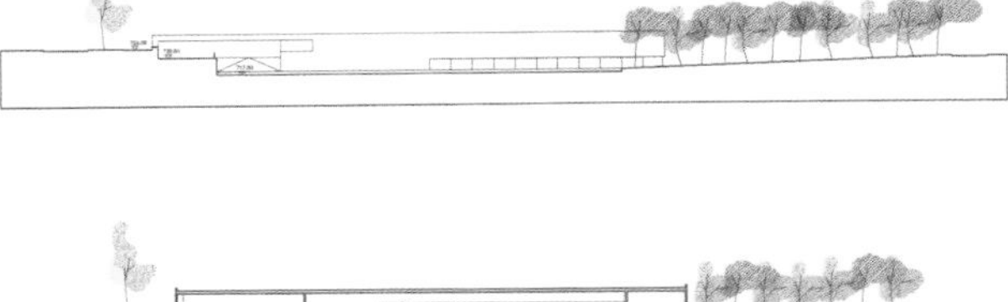

The project responds well to the main stipulation of the competition. Entries were to respond "basically to a reflection on the meaning of a park of these dimensions within the structure of an urban nucleus, from the contemporary perspective, although on the understanding that a park today, like at any other time in history, is not merely an episodic succession of elements but rather the construction of a space to be enjoyed by visitors through the use of tectonic, aquatic and plant elements."

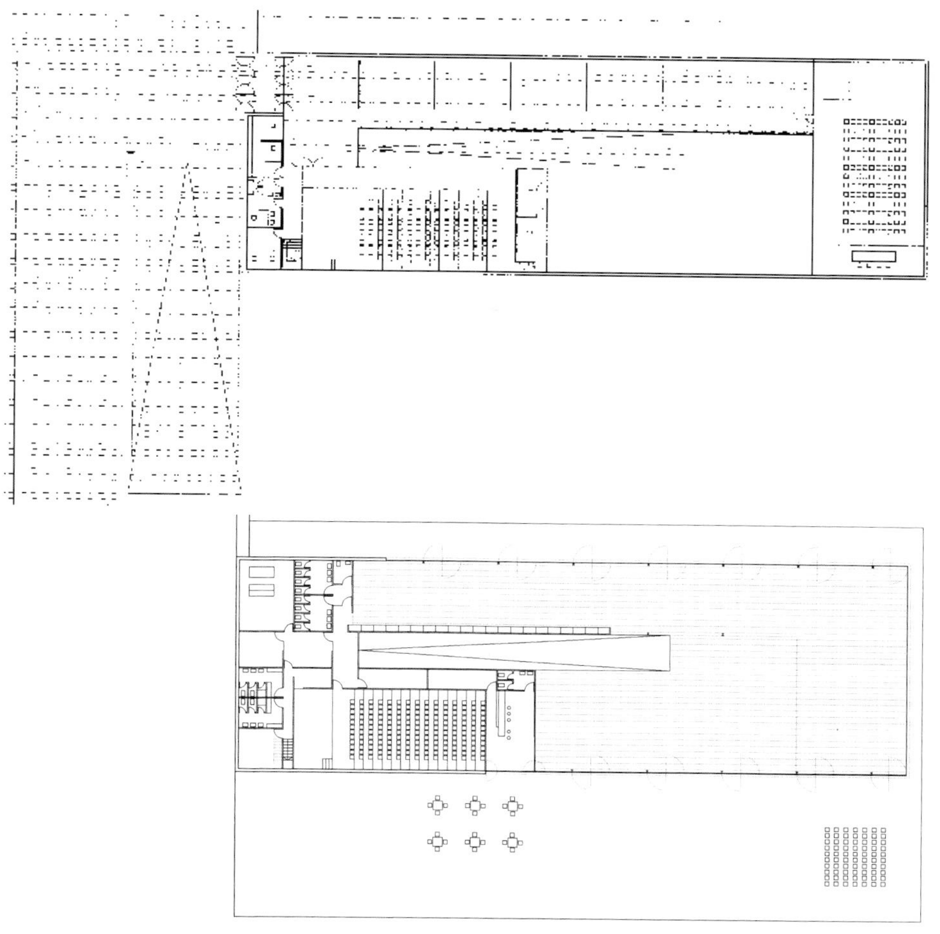

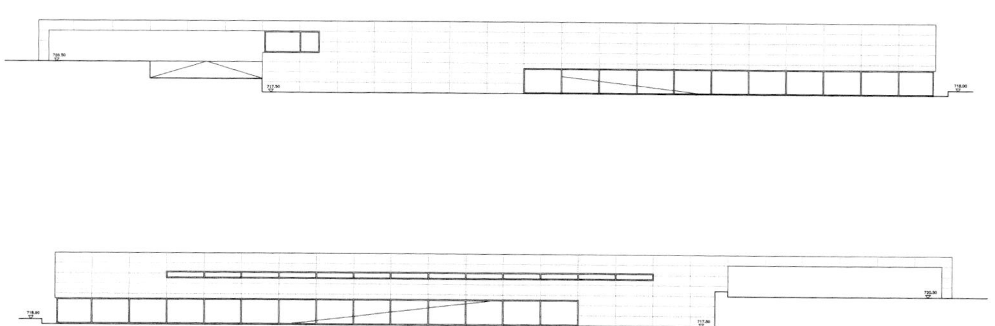

The building equates the ground between the park and the avenue. A porch stands as the access to the building and the main entrance of the park. The rooms, the auditorium, the conference room and the access to the lower floor are distributed along the upper floor. The ground floor consists of an exhibition room: a large space closely related to the park in a physical and perceptive way

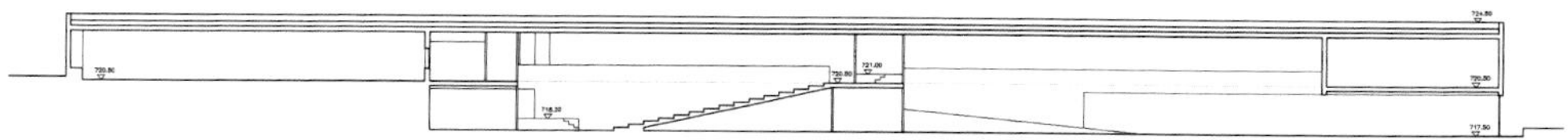

Barcelona Botanical Gardens

Carles Ferrater

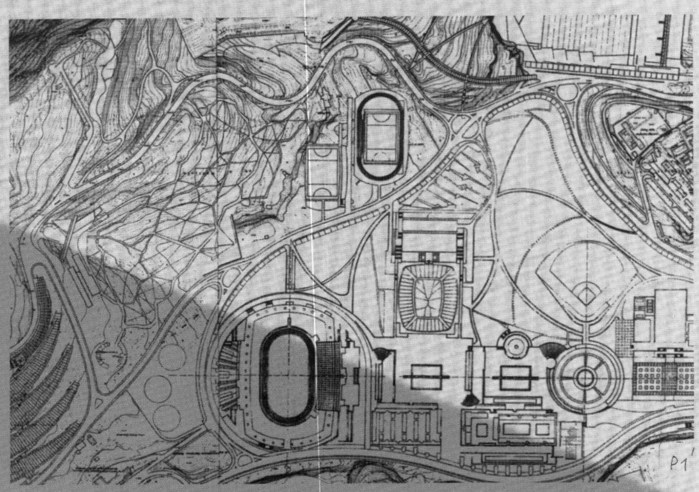

Location: **Barcelona, Spain**

Client: **City Hall of Barcelona**

Construction date: **1999**

Architect: **Carles Ferrater**

Collaborators: **Beth Figueras, José Luís Canosa**

Photography: **Alejo Baguer, Tavisa. Jordi Todó, Estudio Carles Ferrater**

The Barcelona Botanical Gardens
materialize theoretical developments
that are superimposed over the land
in order to create a web of
landscaped spaces and trails

Fragmented Landscape Construction

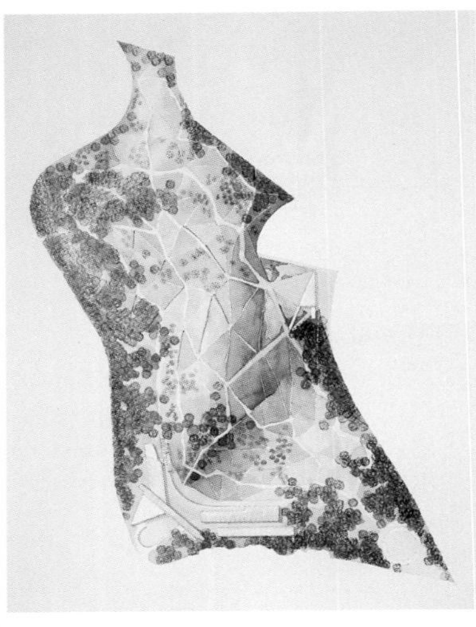

A multi-disciplinary team made up of botanists, landscape designers, and architects designed the Barcelona Botanical Gardens, set on Montjuic's hillside. Two main considerations guided the effort. The first was to establish a pattern that would allow the site itself to set the standard for the design. The idea was that the new landscape would emerge from its own topography. This strategy is quite different from some of the other interventions on Montjuic, many of which failed to respect the mountain's topography and existing forms. Previous projects excavated the mountain, cut the land and inserted plazas and esplanades on the top and hillsides.

The second consideration was related to the configuration of the new garden. Along with Mediterranean flora, it was to include plantings from other international locations with similar climates: California and part of Japan from the Northern Hemisphere, and parts of Chile, South Africa, and a small coastal region in Australia from the Southern Hemisphere.

The layout for the new gardens is based on botanical and ecological aspects, and attempts to blend the shapes of the plants on display. The gardens are, from this point of view, a valuable scientific tool. From this sprang the idea to draw a triangular mesh over the land. The mesh adapts to every topographical contour, unraveling at the edges, and expanding or contracting according to the slope. It follows the three main directions of the contour lines, so that the vortex of every triangle is the same height, and with almost no incline. Other subdivisions of the mesh relate to accessibility and plantations.

This irregular and variable geometric order, adapted to the terrain, allows optimization of the hidden infrastructures, like water and drainage lines. It also permits classification of the itineraries according to their use and their slant, establishing primary, secondary, and maintenance paths. Since it facilitates the mosaic-like arrangement of the diverse vegetation, it also organizes the territory for scientific, pedagogic, and leisure uses. Future structures like greenhouses, nurseries, shade shelters, and research and services facilities will follow the same plan.

If the height of the triangle vortexes is altered slightly, the mesh starts to fracture and the land becomes faceted. Then, every part of the whole has a unique incline and orientation, and relates separately to needs of water, cultivation, and proximity to the other varieties of its type. The mesh is fractured by groups of double triangular walls, concave or convex, that show a variation in height, length, and curvature. With them, the landscape acquires a fractionated order and dimension. In other words, a harmonious aspect results from irregularity and fragmentation. Later on, the plant growth will create a new order that will fuse with the initial proposal, attenuating any excessive abstraction of the project. This method, so artificial in the beginning, ends up assimilating itself into nature's fragmented dimension. Logic and harmonic order are achieved from seemingly chaotic and diverse components.

The project's logic doesn't depend on any specific scale or a predetermined configuration. The garden's final size does not affect its reach. It is the triangular mesh that organizes the landscape and solves the project's complex demands.

Duisburg-Nord Park

Latz and Partners

Location: **Duisburg, Nordrhein-Westfalen, Germany**

Client: **Development Company of Nordrhein-Westfalen and the city of Duisburg**

Construction date: **1991-2000**

Architects: **Latz and Partners**

Collaborators: **IBA (Internationale Bauaustellung), IG Nordpark,**
Society for Industrial Culture and the Parks Department of Duisburg City Council

Photographs: **Latz & Partner, Christa Panick, Peter Wilde, Michael Latz and Angus Parker**

Old Industrial Areas Become City Parks

This project for Duisburg-Nord Park forms part of a huge green zone in the region of Emscher and was developed for the International Architecture Exhibition of 1999. The German Federal State of Nordrhein-Westfalen and various cities in the region of Emscher have initiated several projects with the ultimate goal of refurbishing old industrial areas in the Ruhr basin.

The Duisburg-Nord Park is situated between the cities of Meiderich and Hamborn in a zone of heavy industries (coal and steel) between the urban agglomerations of Duisburg and Oberhausen in the Ruhr basin. With a population of five million inhabitants, the area is one of the country's major industrial zones. The former site of the Thyssen foundry has preserved all the paraphernalia that is so typical of the industry: a smelting furnace, warehouses, and rail installations, now in disuse.

Latz & Partners won the 1990 international competition to update the area and provide its dense population with recreational, sports and cultural amenities.

The project revives the landscape and the old industrial installations. It respects the complex's important historical value and treats it as an archaeological window into the coal and the steel industries. The intervention preserves the remains of the old installations as valuable heritage, and makes them available for public enjoyment. The enormous structures are now landmarks in their own right. One of the initial ideas was to turn them into integral elements of the park, places to be used and enjoyed by the residents.

The fragmented, rundown structures were never meant to be reconstructed. They present certain independent systems whose connections could be functional in some cases and visual in others. The systems are connected by a railway park with raised walkways, an aquatic park in the lowest part and promenades that link the park with various city districts. Other elements, like small gardens, terraces, towers, footbridges and plazas, connect the larger zones.

The magnitude of the project called for piece-by-piece interventions that are opened to the public as they are completed. As much as possible, on-site materials have been used, both directly, and recycled, as in the case of the iron in the footbridges, platforms and gates. Other materials have been used for paving or for mixing concrete for the new walls. The huge hematite sheets that cover the ground of the Piazza Metallica were taken from the smelting furnaces.

The elements which have been developed to date are the footbridges connecting different parts of the park, certain stretches of the system of water courses, gardens and patios occupied by the old mineral deposits, and certain spots such as Cowper Place, Piazza Metallica, the theater and Stonehall Place which occupy characteristic sites in the factory's construction system. Separate gardens have been laid out with a variety of plant life. Local inhabitants have participated by planting small box-gardens that reuse waste materials from the production process in order to study possible types of vegetation that could be planted in the park.

The mineral deposit gardens are built at different levels. Their walls are two meters thick and had to be perforated to provide access to them

On the following page:
Piazza Metallica. This singular spot reveals the potential for metamorphosis of factory installations. A quiet square surrounded by yards of piping, tanks and chimneys provides space for vegetation. The paving in the center, makes good use of huge sheets of hematite, each weighing over seven tons, originally part of the smelting furnaces

The aquatic park. A canal, which uses the bed of an old main drain, crosses the park from east to west. A network of clean water is provided for the various gardens, using wind-powered energy

y in domestic architecture

domestic architecture

gy in domestic archi

ecology

cology in domestic architecture

ecology in domestic arc

gy in domestic architecture

in domestic architecture

ogy in domestic arch

ecology in domestic architecture

ecology in domestic ar

ecology in dome

y in domestic architecture

ecology in dom

ecology in domestic arc

hitecture

ure

ecture

omestic architecture

tecture

ture

chitecture

ecology in domestic architecture

ture

tecture

itecture

architecture

ture

tic architecture

tecture

Four Horizons

Lindsay Johnston

Location: Watagan Forest, Hunter Valley, Australia

Client: Foundation Four Horizons

Construction date: 1998

Architect: Lindsay Johnston

Collaborators: Su Johnston, Robert White

Photography: Peter Hyatt, Michael Nicholson

The Four Horizons home is outstanding in its energy conservation. Subtracting solar contribution and wood burning, its net usage of energy is approximately one third of the average.

The Self-sufficient Residence

The Four Horizons Residence towers over a cliff in the midst of a eucalyptus forest – the Watagan State Forest – recently designated as a National Park. Located 150 kilometers north of Sydney, the site is 430 meters above sea level with spectacular views over the Hunter River Valley.

A holistic conception is essential to this project. The isolated enclave of the residence and the absence of public utilities (water, electricity, sewer or phone) suggest that designer and client were inclined to reach forth by experimenting with extreme conditions. If self-sufficiency was not thoroughly contemplated, the house was doomed to fail. Consequently, the site is manipulated so that its self-regulating processes will not damage human interests. From this standpoint, the house wasn't placed trying to "protect" nature – she fends for herself – but to organize the sustainability of human presence.

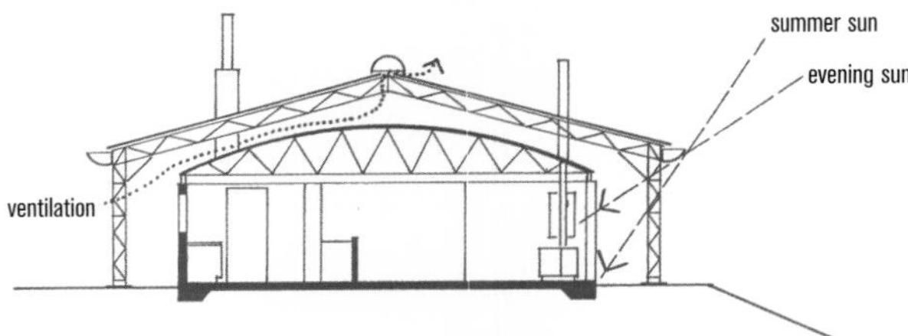

This brings new challenges to the house since it must obtain, control and manage its own energy sources. The approach is to reconcile activities with low environmental impact, to use readily available materials and technology, and to recycle the waste produced. Water is supplied by rain collection. Solar energy is used for water heating, generating electricity, and for charging the radio (phone/fax/e-mail). The orientation and the construction solutions allow for natural climate control. Wood burning is used for heating and cooking. The residual waste is treated and sent back to the environment, with the knowledge that it will not affect the surroundings.

The house sits parallel to the cliffs in order to benefit from the morning sun in the winter and the cooling breeze in the summer, since it turns its back on the stronger winds. On the exterior, we find a series of solar panels, generators, and the garage and stables that open onto an enclosed garden forming a patio.

The covering of the house is resolved with a freestanding double-sloping roof. As is typical with many Australian barns and agricultural warehouses, a steel structure with galvanized metal is used. The first roof is separated from the living space in order to regulate ventilation and temperature, and to control the entrance of light. It also works as a great surface for shade and water collection. The collected water is stored in tanks with a much greater capacity (600 liters) than is needed for daily use, which guarantees a reserve for many months.

Under this shed, two habitable modules with curved metallic sub-roofs accommodate, on one side, the common areas – living, dining, kitchen, and pantry – and on the other, a study, bedrooms, and bathrooms. An outdoor hallway separates the two units for greater thermal efficiency and sound/activities isolation.

The construction solutions are adequate for the thermal conditions of the different dispositions. While the concrete walls are exposed inside, they are sheathed on the outside with polyester wool insulation, steel mini-spheres, and eucalyptus planks to implement a thermal shield.

These conditions – together with the physical properties and the distinct handling of other elements like the shutters, the shed, the perforated bricks, the outdoor corridor, and the outbuildings – produce an efficient thermal response from the house, which remains 10°C cooler than the outside in summer and the reverse in winter.

Within the traditional context of the Australian single family residence, this house stands out for its energy conservation. In Four Horizons, the positioning, orientation, selection of materials, construction methods, and the careful management of resources and waste were all brought together by an integral concept.

The double covering allows for ventilation of the interior living spaces and regulates temperature and lighting. Water is collected in large tanks that can provide water reserves for many months.

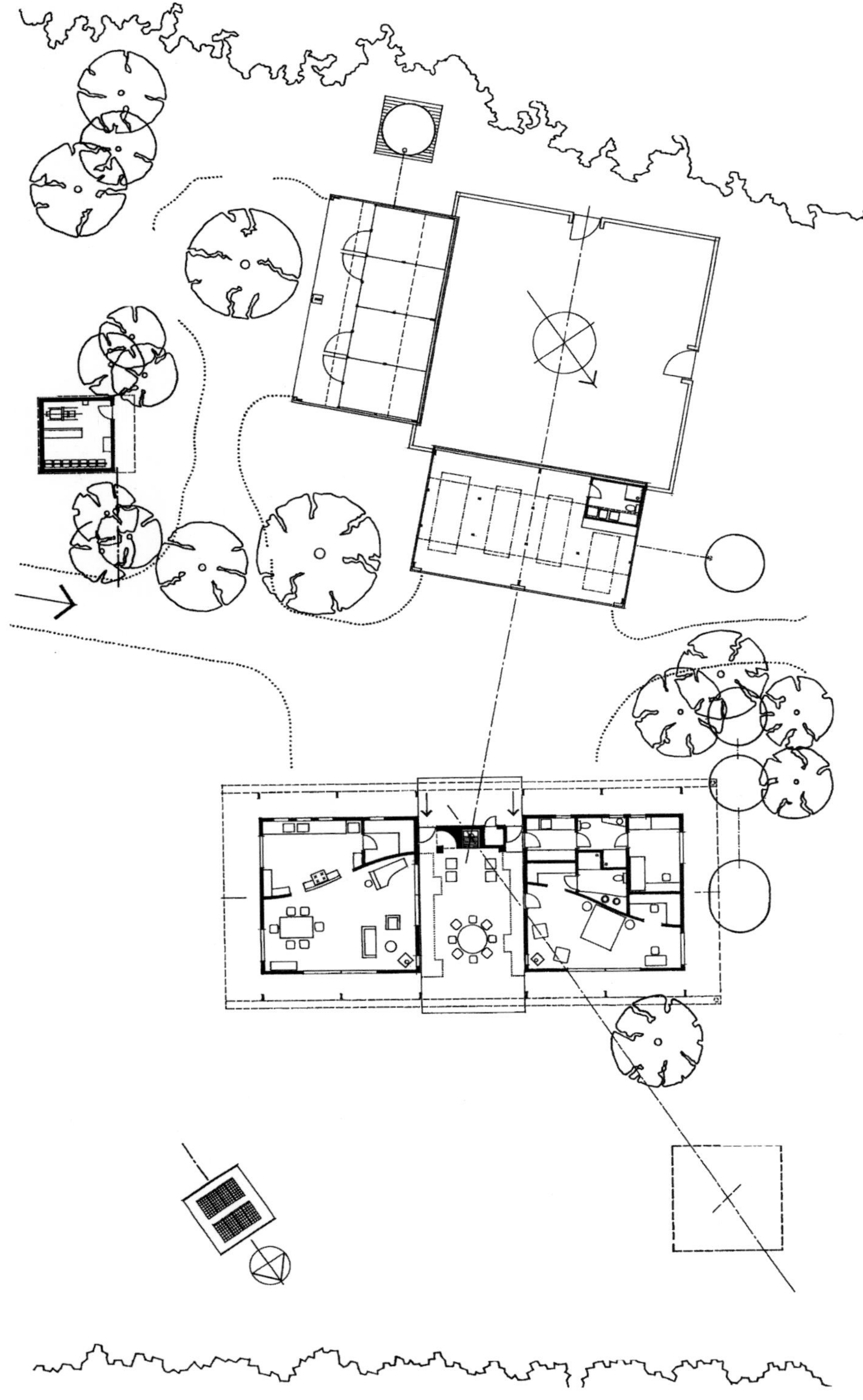

The site plan shows the residence with its living spaces and adjacent structures that include barns, a greenhouse, and a garage. The water tanks and generators occupy small structures on the lot

The interiors are also specifically designed to profit from the thermal conditions particular to each season. The result is temperature differences up to 10°C from the exterior

A House in Lauterach

Walter Unterrainer

Location: **Lauterach, Austria**

Client: **Ratz/Streisslberg**

Construction date: **1997**

Architect: **Walter Unterrainer**

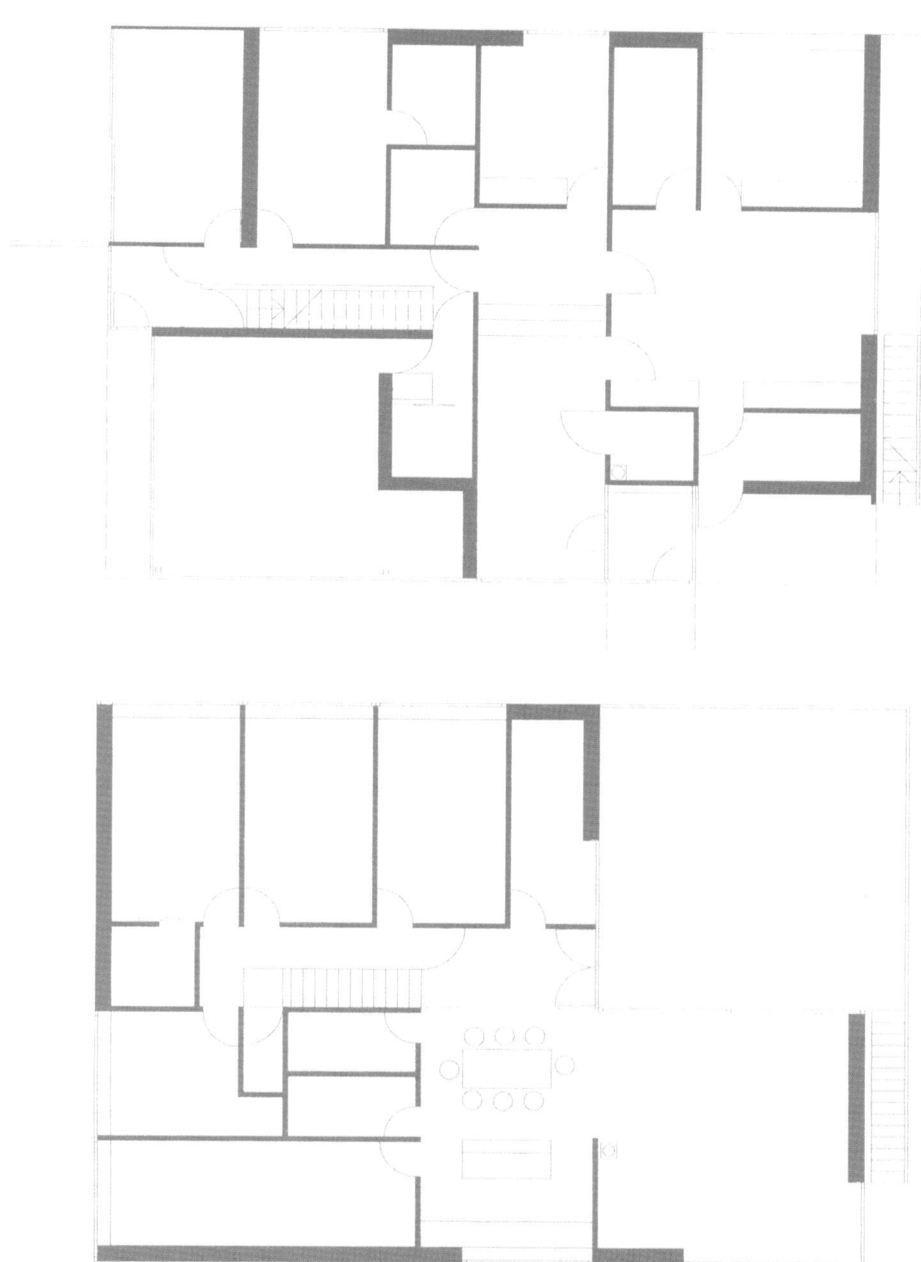

The Elementary as a Model of Efficiency

The single-family dwelling is the ideal framework for an architect to take certain liberties in the design process. Houses of this kind are generally isolated structures in natural settings that require a substantial degree of responsibility on the part of the designer. In the case of this house in Lauterach, Austria, the design was required to combine two different uses – a doctor's office and home – in an area of extreme climatic conditions. The site is surrounded and tempered by both urban and rural references. Walter Unterrainer, the architect designer, has managed to come up with a project that responds to a set of multiple, mutually antagonistic factors. The result is a unitary project characterized by simple lines and a high degree of energy efficiency.

The proportions of the house were designed keeping in mind the most characteristic aspects of the site. The property is on the borderline of the city and country. The architect decided to place the house and its entrance towards the lot's southwestern side, which runs onto the densely developed Mäder Street. In this way, the dwelling is inserted into the urban tissue by means of an almost blind façade in keeping with the predominant morphology of the sector. Toward the east, the façade opens towards the magnificent views of the mountain and valley. Two elements that strongly influence the site are the VKW Tower, which stands on the site, and two old walnut trees that grow there. On its western side, the house relates to the rear façade of the tower by means of the parking lot open to the street. This point of urban reference is thereby exploited through the creation of a surface that is not hermetically closed to traffic.

Given the program's twofold functional requirements of the program, the doctor's medical practice on one hand and the parking lot and dwelling on the other, Unterrainer decided to create a single coherent volume so as not to overdevelop the site and cause its deterioration. Most of the site was set aside for the garden, while the compact volume of the house accommodates the two functions. The medical office is on the ground floor beside the parking lot, while the house as such is on the floor above, beneath the existing treetops and with the best views of the surrounding landscape. Behind its clear, restful appearance, the compact volume contains multiple articulations that make possible different relationships with the surroundings, including cross ventilation and double illumination of the interior spaces. The flat roof does not appear as a huge mass imposed on the site.

The house's structure is based on a prefabricated modular system that reduces costs and makes for easier construction. Nonetheless, the project is striking due to its use of inexpensive glass on the façades and exterior facing panels. This material generates a unified skin and makes it possible to adapt the construction to the thermal conditions of each of the different orientations. The local climate is characterized by low temperatures from early fall until late spring. On the north façade, the glass acts as the facing for a conventionally ventilated and insulated wall. On the east and west façades and on the blind sections of the south wall, black-painted cellular cardboard has been placed behind the conventionally ventilated glass. The result is similar to that of a heat-collecting wall, but without the cost and difficulties normally involved with this kind of structure. It also provides a cool interior during the summer.

The symmetrical composition of the main body and the way in which the façades have been treated are two aspects that create a unified image and achieve high energy efficiency, without the need to apply highly developed technologies. It is an almost elementary project that responds intelligently to all aspects of its surroundings without overlooking the main function of the home: the comfort of its occupants.

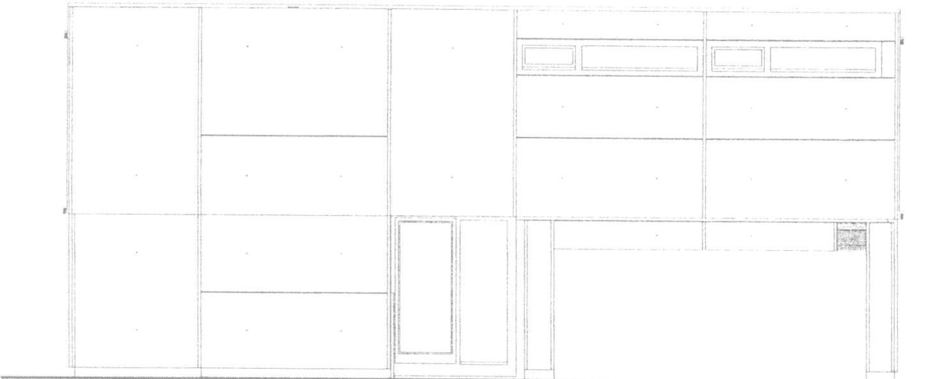

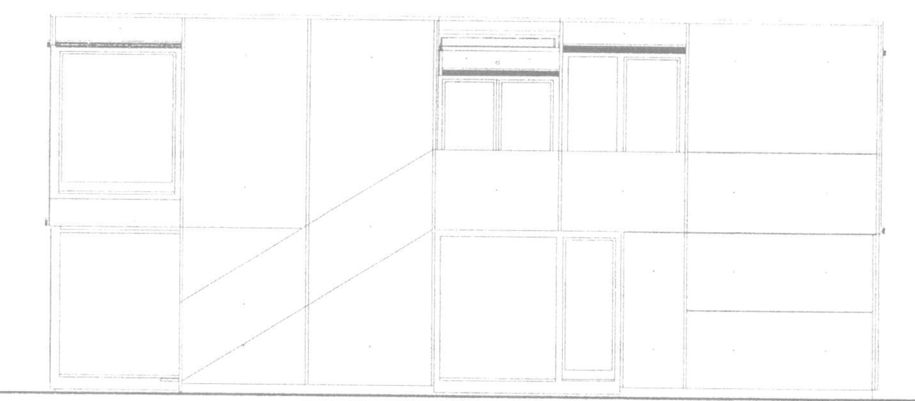

The location of the building and the tower clearly divides the exterior space into a preliminary public zone and a private green zone. The appropriate volumetric articulation of the house made it possible to fully exploit the exterior spaces and enhance the views from inside

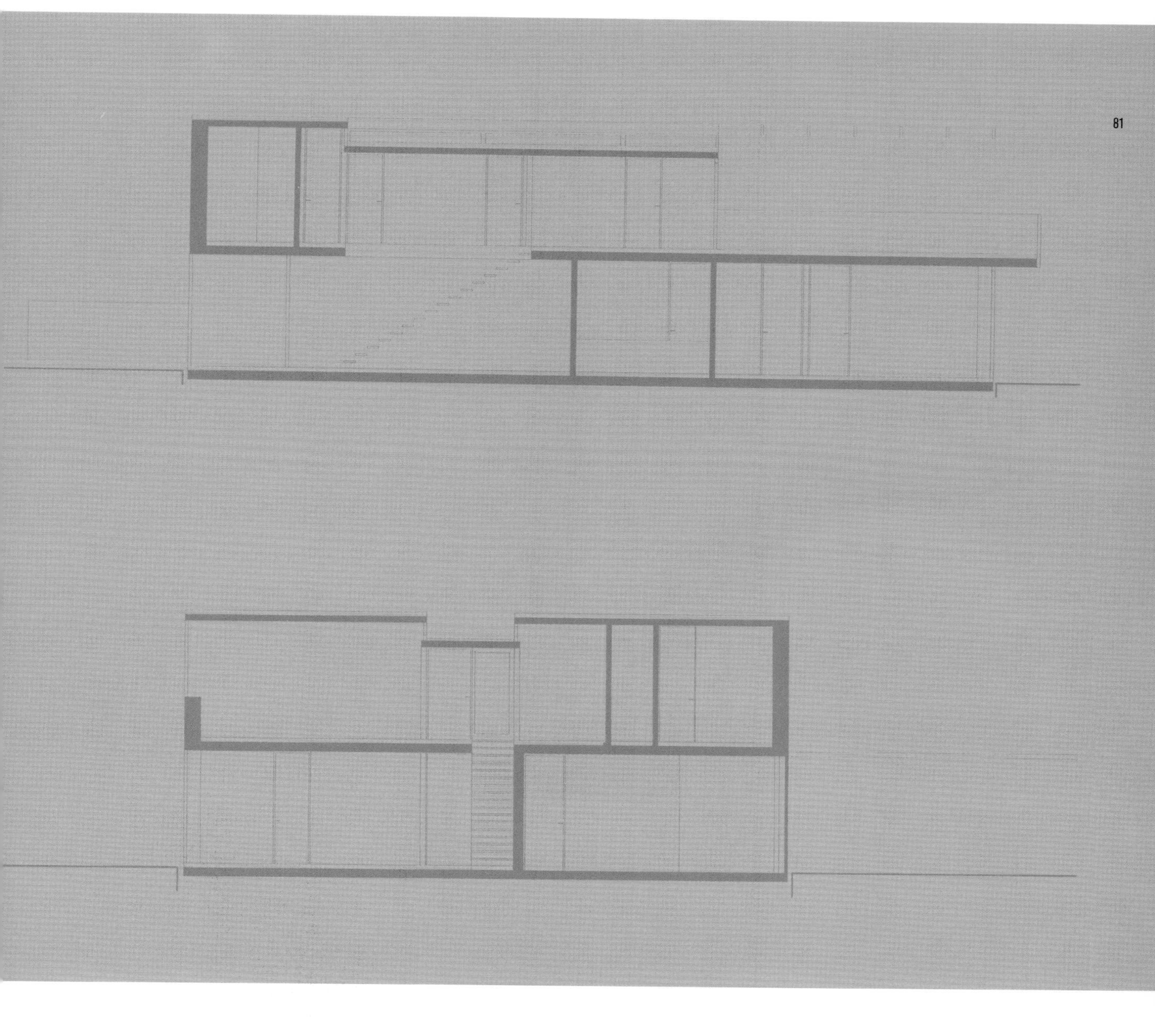

"Forest House" Exhibition Pavilion

Michael Jockers

Location: **Stuttgart, Germany**

Client: **Land Baden - Württemberg**

Construction date: **1997**

Architect: **Michael Jockers**

Collaborators: **Rosemarie Wagner**

Photography: **Martin Duckek**

The images from the Michael Jockers Pavilion show a variety of fenestrations and wall finishes; every façade is specific to its requirements, whether it is energy conservation or capturing the views of the adjacent forest through transparency

Energy Efficiency

The Exhibition Pavilion uses the formal expressivity of this type of building as an architectural resource to achieve integration with the landscape and energy efficiency. The Forest House intends, through teaching programs, to create an emotional relationship with Nature by activating sensory perception. This is accomplished through self-invented tests, investigation, and experimentation, while keeping in mind the characteristics of the surroundings. Accordingly, a number of the learning programs are conducted in the forests surrounding the house.

The project is located near the city, not far from the Stuttgart Television Tower, in the midst of a municipal forest with great outdoor living potential. The building's main aspiration is to emphasize the connection between the exhibition on the inside and the woods on the outside. The relationship between the building and its environment is already apparent in the distribution of the Pavilion's activities. The program includes flexible exhibition areas, a conference room, and a do-it-yourself workshop. The elements controlling the technical aspects for the house are located in the core of the first floor. The central positioning of the stairs allows short routes and easy orientation. An open gallery leading to the first floor rooms offers an overview of the exhibition area below and panoramic vistas of the surrounding woods.

The building is shaped by two distinguishable volumes, set against each other in form, that closely relate to the activities taking place in the interior, as much as to the exterior. The smaller rooms, intended as workshops and administrative areas, are located in the two-story volume and partition the building's shell as needed. Some sections are closed-in and covered with untreated wood and some are opened by paneled windows.

The glass exhibit area is the element possessing the most formal expressiveness. It appears as a counterpoint and makes possible the observation of the circumventing forest and its changing influence over the seasons. The filigree type of construction is made of multi-laminated wood and arches over the flexible-use area of the project.

The use of conifer wood from the vicinity of Ulm in framing both volumes illustrates a complex system of forest exploitation and the resulting preservation of non-renewable reserves. The contrast between the two volumes, one compact and the other transparent, reveals to the visitor the purpose of the construction and its function in relation to the exterior.

The architectural design suggests formal eloquence and an adequate and complete environmental conception that is adapted to the works of construction. The two-story compact volume is well insulated, while the exhibition hall, with its wide fenestration, functions as a solar room and works as a heating or cooling device, depending on the season. During summer, the roofing unfolds a double covering that has two functions. It reflects most of the sunlight, which prevents overheating, and acts as a "solar chimney," by extracting the heat accumulated on the interior and directing it through the double sheathing to the upper part of the roof.

During winter, the double cover folds during the day. An opening on the top closes to let in light and heat. This system acts as a natural heater for the rest of the building. "Solar walls" make the process even more efficient and provide insulation in summer and heat retention in winter. The project also has an active solar energy system over the roof of the exhibition area. The photovoltaic installation is connected to the electric system and is meant to supply the remaining energy needed for water heating or additional climate control. Only 15 percent of the cells´ total capacity is used for the project´s basic needs; the remaining 85 percent is introduced into the local utility network against a bonus payment. The ensemble reacts to its surroundings, the weather, and the seasons. The result is a model for the concept of the "low energy consumption building."

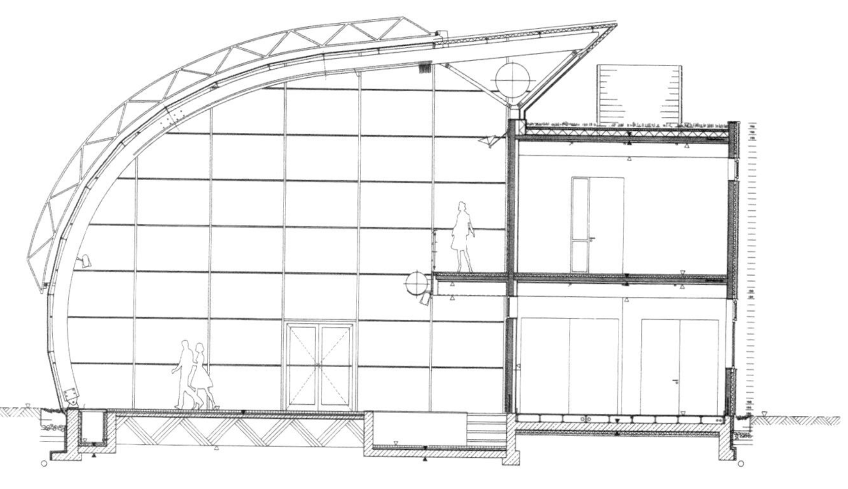

The different mechanisms implemented to make the building consume the least possible energy can be appreciated throughout the different graphic representations–sections, sketches, and floor plans. Its relationship with Nature is perceptive and bioclimatic

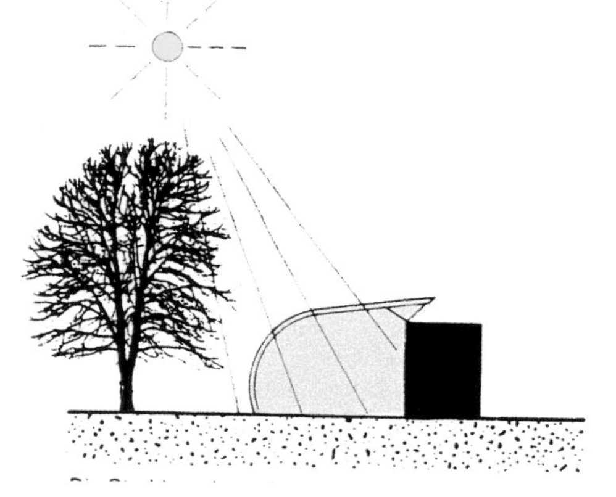

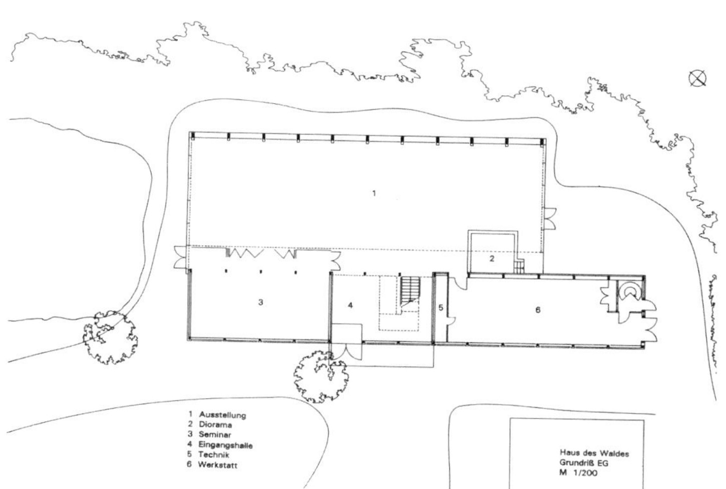

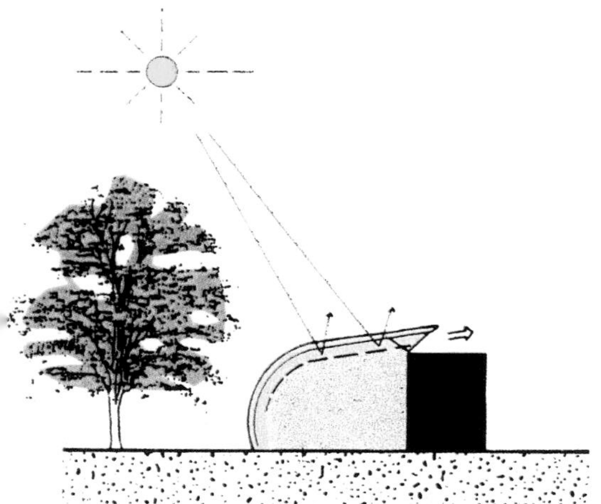

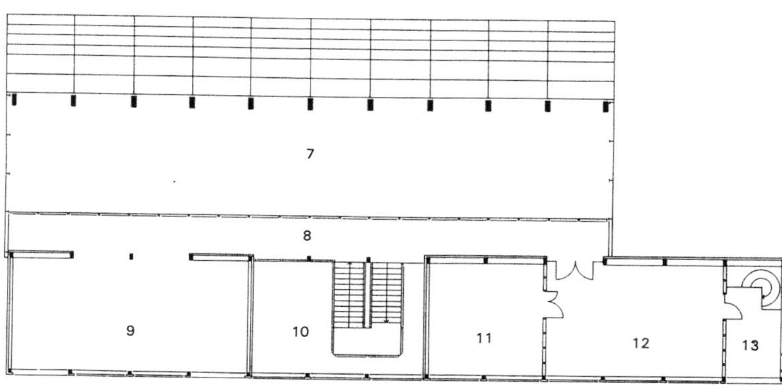

A House in Draguignan

Bertrand Bonnier

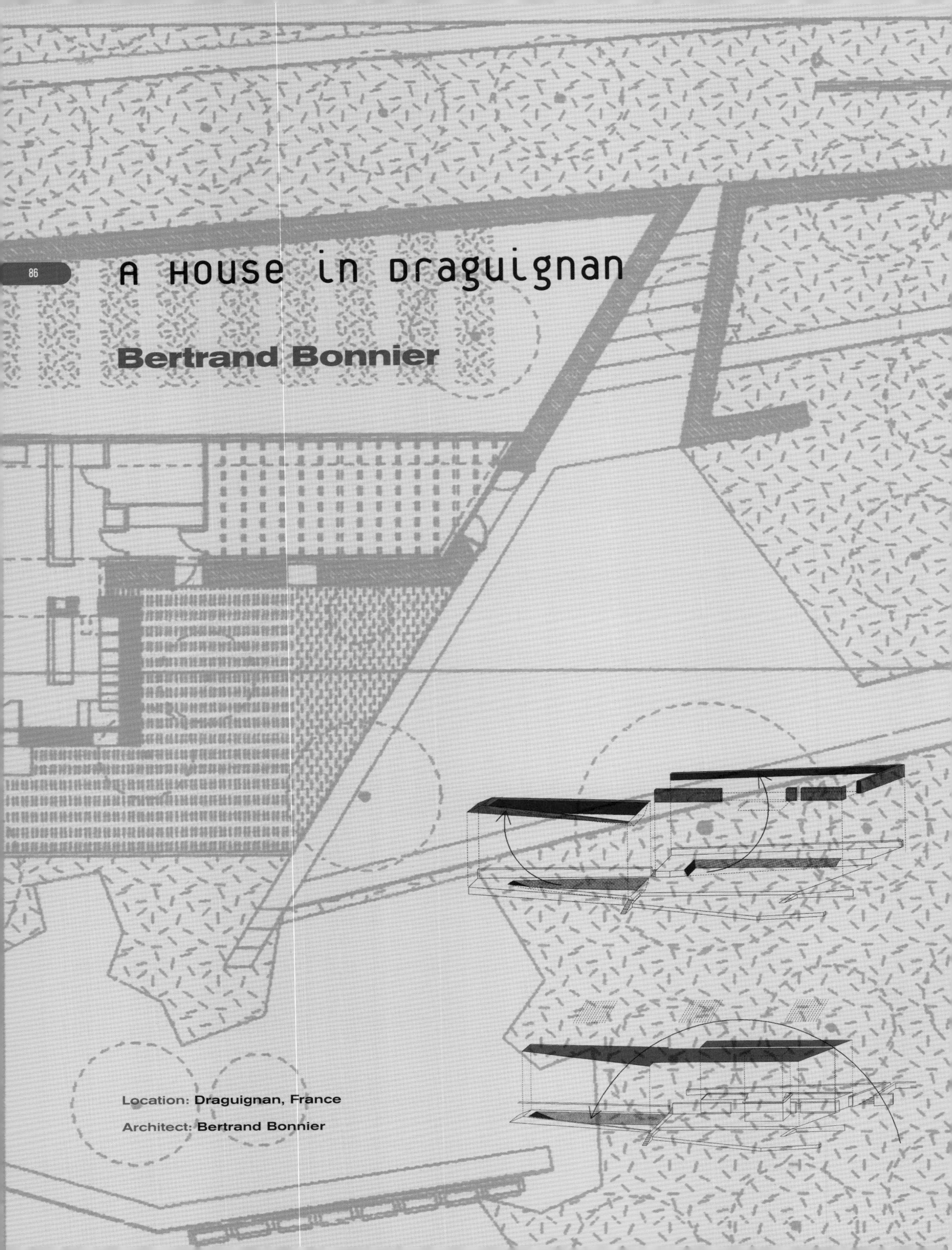

Location: **Draguignan, France**

Architect: **Bertrand Bonnier**

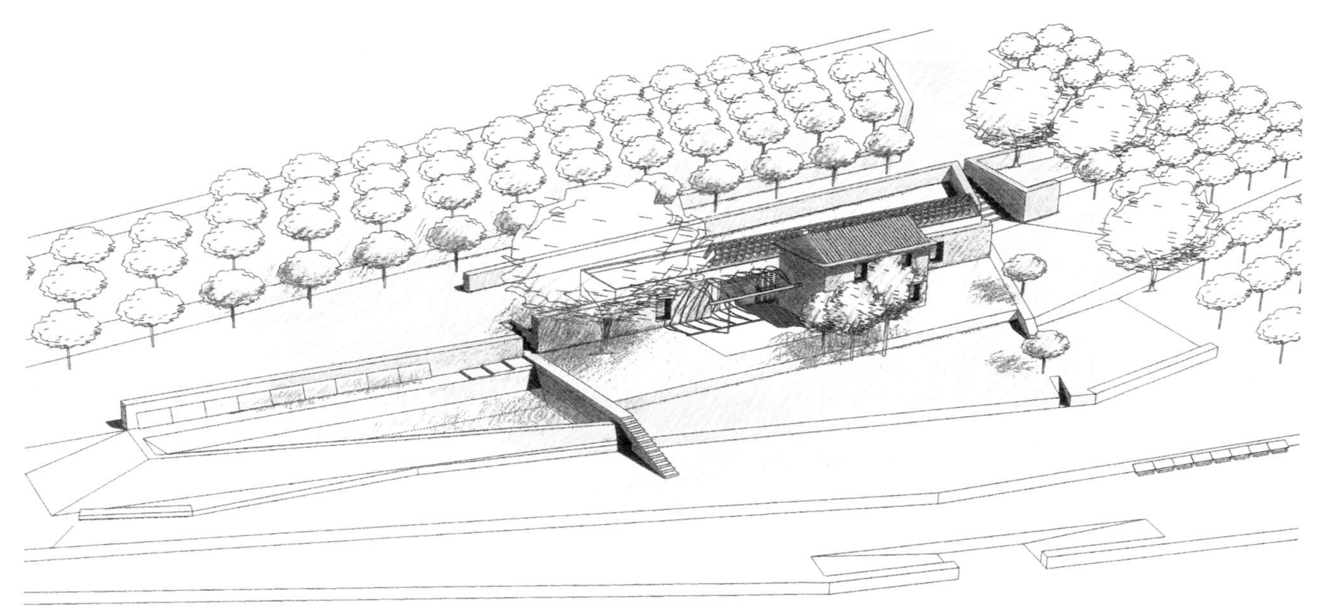

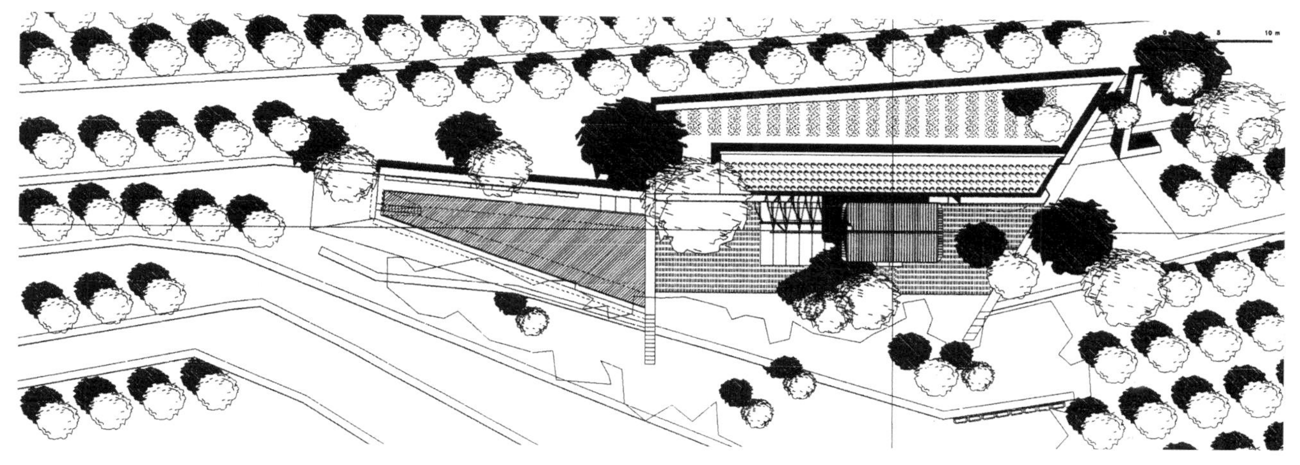

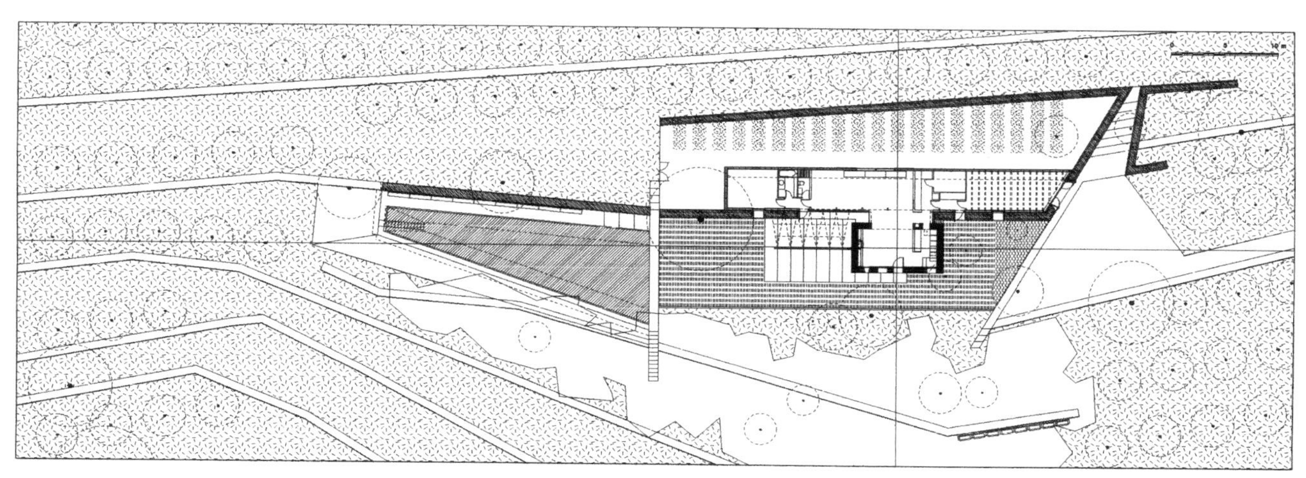

A Project Born of the Earth

The interest that arose a few decades ago in different approaches to landscaping, and recent research into the exploitation of energy resources, have resulted in projects that establish an interactive dialogue between architecture and place. In general, this relationship has been perceived as a phenomenon in which the landscape includes architecture. This project by Bertrand Bonnier for a house near Draguignan inverts the order so that the construction includes the landscape. This inversion of concepts required a detailed, responsible approach to the elements comprising the surroundings. Bonnier´s project highlights a necessary virtue of the architect when it comes to such interventions: humility.

This project's origins are not architectural, constructional or even aesthetic. On one hand, it poses questions regarding the future of a rural landscape and, on the other, sets out to revive and give new blood to something that was dead. The venture began four years ago with the search for a secluded rural site in the Provence-Alpes-Côte d'Azur region that would fulfill the requirements for this type of intervention. The arduous task of finding such a specific place involved long walks through the countryside and the meticulous study of detailed maps and aerial photographs. The compiled data revealed the area's seasonal variations and plant cycles. Such a detailed study of the landscape is representative of this project, a minute search for the thread of a timeless fabric.

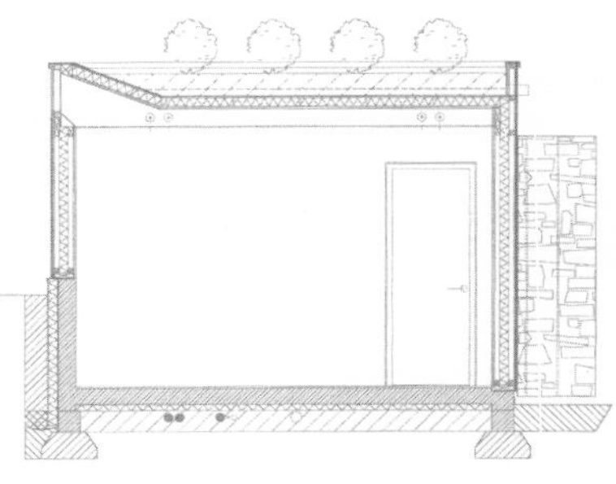

With the collaboration of agricultural and forestry commissions, olive trees were planted, after having first been carefully selected to ensure the profitability of the plantation. Bonnier studied the sunlight, hail, wind, rainfall, and subsoil and conducted experiments to find the most suitable tree species for the area by considering their germination, size, behavior, and appearance outside the harvesting season. Another important consideration was water management, either from springs or descending from the forests.

This return to the region's remote past would take a long time. Meanwhile, a house was needed so that more attention could be devoted to working the land. The architectural project started with a modest, rudimentary building. The architect devised a volumetric strategy that exalts the intrinsic values of the existing building. Behind it, a long brick building was constructed with a water tank at its western end. The house itself cultivates the roots from which it was born in an avid search for past resonances. Thus, the project is presented as an installation on the site, which includes stone walls filled with local earth, planted terraces and rocky gardens.

The project and its formal architectural repertoire include the presence of rainwater, wind, sun, the shade produced by the trees, and all the constituent elements of the place. The timber structure is clad in panels of the same material and attached by means of an insulating layer of polystyrene. The blinds control the penetration of direct sunlight, while the roof garden maintains an even temperature inside during both the day and the night. A set of photovoltaic panels will be installed on the top part of the roof to meet supplementary energy requirements. These carefully thought out devices are integrated almost invisibly into the structure. The whole installation considers the needs of contemporary comfort and ensures the house's energy efficiency in harmony with the landscape.

History, agriculture, and landscape constitute the very life of this project and the elements that provide the architecture with its specific weight. It is a contemporary version of old constructions that resulted from perfect knowledge of the site. Like these houses, it has the ability to settle into the ground, reemerge, and take advantage of the natural elements. There is no mimicry here, nor transparency, nor ostentation; the house follows guidelines based on an acute sense of responsibility.

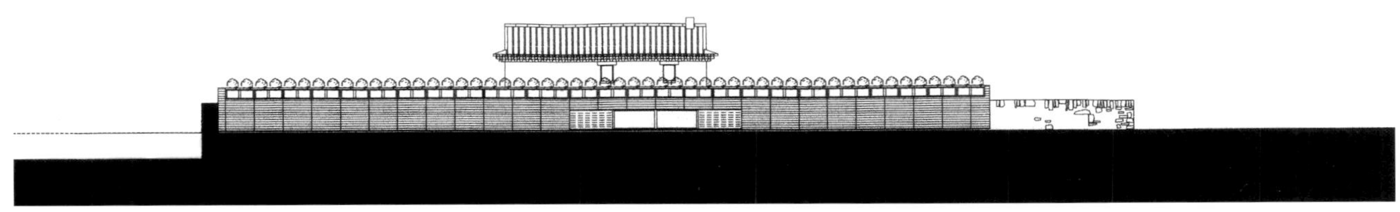

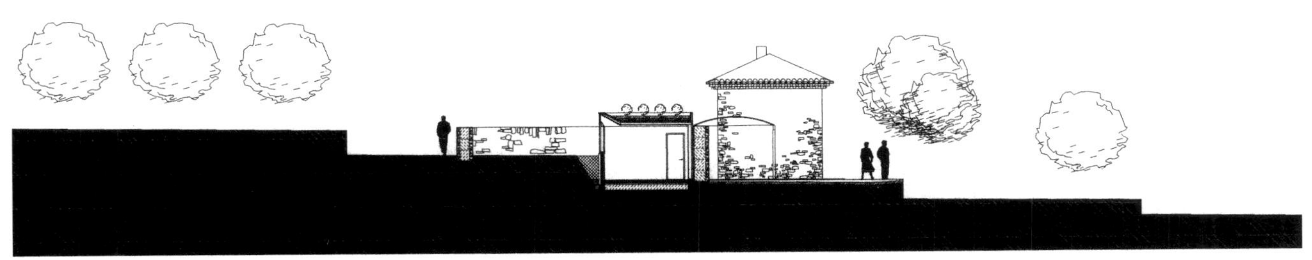

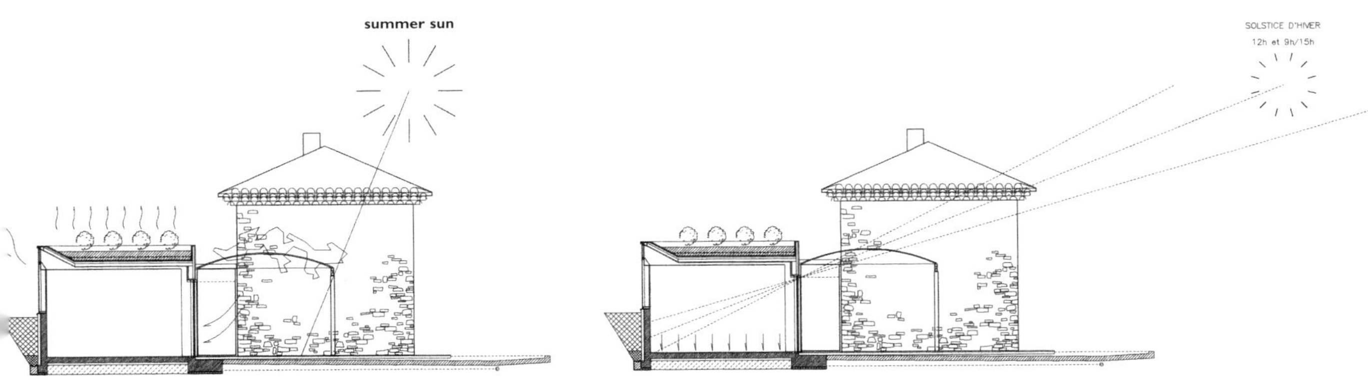

The project pays special attention to working the land. The architectural or aesthetic principles have been applied to regenerate the rural landscape

The house takes advantage of different natural elements. The roof features solar panels and a garden, both designed to foster the project's thermal inertia

From technology to nature

the evolution of high-tech

the evolution of
the evolution of high-tech
the evolution of high-
the evolution of hig
the evol
evolution of high-tech
the evolution of high-tech
the evolution of
he evolution of high-
the evolution of high-tech
the evolution of
the evolution of high-tech
the evolution of high
the evolution of hi
evolution of high-tech
the evolution of high-tech
the evolution of
the ev
the evolution of high
the evolution of high-tech
e evolution of high-tech
the evolut
the evolution of h
the evolution of high-tech

the evolution of high-tech

alterations to the Reichstag

Foster & Partners

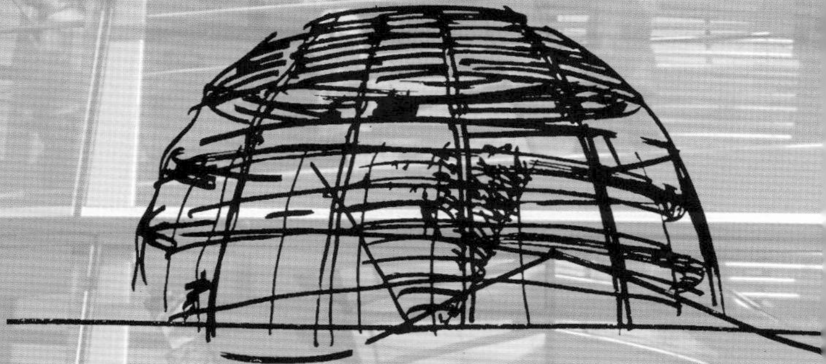

Location: **Berlin, Germany**

Client: **Bundesrepublik Deutschland**

Construction date: **1999**

Architects: **Foster & Partners**

Collaborators: **David Nelson, Mark Braun, Dieter Muller, Ingo Pott**

Photographs: **Dennis Gilbert, Nigel Young**

Light, Ventilation and Natural Air-Conditioning: Traces of the Reichstag

This project is fruit of the initiative to move the German parliament from Bonn to Berlin and to rehouse it in the Reichstag. A competition was convened in 1992 for the construction of an area of 353,500 square feet, almost 100% more than the Reichstag could contain. Subsequently, the total area was reduced to about 96,000 square feet. The teams initially selected were those of Pi de Bruijn, Santiago Calatrava, and Norman Foster. After further deliberation on the part of the jury, Foster & Partners won the contest.

The project consisted in designing a plenary hall inside the Reichstag – a building officially inaugurated in 1894, burnt in 1933, partially destroyed in 1945, restored in the sixties, and "hidden" in 1995. The complexity of the initial brief was further increased by the posteriori decision to modify the building's environmental qualities. This involved designing an energy-efficient structure that would generate its own heat and reduce the emission of pollutant residues.

The reconstructed building reflects the clear idea of the old Reichstag. The basis of the project was the original building, and a major operation had to be carried out to reveal its "skeleton". Transparency and accessibility were the keys to the reconstruction of the Reichstag´s interior. Today, an ordinary visitor who enters the building from the west may witness a session in parliament and be seen by the parliamentarians.

The main level of the parliament has been moved to the historical first floor, while the second floor contains the chairman's rooms and the Council of Elders. The third floor accommodates the meeting rooms for the different parties and the pressroom. The terrace above these work areas allows the public access to the restaurant and the dome. Inside the dome, two helicoidal ramps lead up to a raised platform from which it is possible to enjoy views of the city.

The new glass dome is the departure point for the interior works, and it opens the building to natural light and views. It is therefore an essential component in the strategies of energy saving and natural illumination. The dome is conceived as a "lantern", with all the possible interpretations that this implies. Its nucleus contains a cone covered with angled mirrors that reflect the light of the horizon inside the building, and a moving protection device that, by following the trajectory of the sun, prevents excessive heating and glare. The dome is also an essential component of the natural ventilation system: the air inside the building is drawn up into it by the chimney effect. In turn, the cone extracts the warm air from the highest levels while the axial ventilators and heat exchangers recycle the energy of the stale air.

The energy that activates the ventilation system, the air outlet, and the devices that shade the building is generated by the panels of photovoltaic cells arranged on the south face of the roof. At the same time, due to the variation in the number of users of the building, it was decided to adopt a flexible energy-saving strategy. A pleasant temperature is supplied depending on which heating or cooling system is activated. This method reduces maximum temperature peaks by 30% compared to traditional methods.

The use of a new system of energy co-generation using palm and sunflower oils reduces the emission of carbon dioxide by 94%. This is significant if one bears in mind that the services supplied with fossil energy installed in the Reichstag in 1960 released the alarming quantity of 7,000 tons of carbon dioxide into the atmosphere per annum. To continue using this system would be the equivalent of using the same amount of energy needed to supply the homes of 5,000 people for one year.

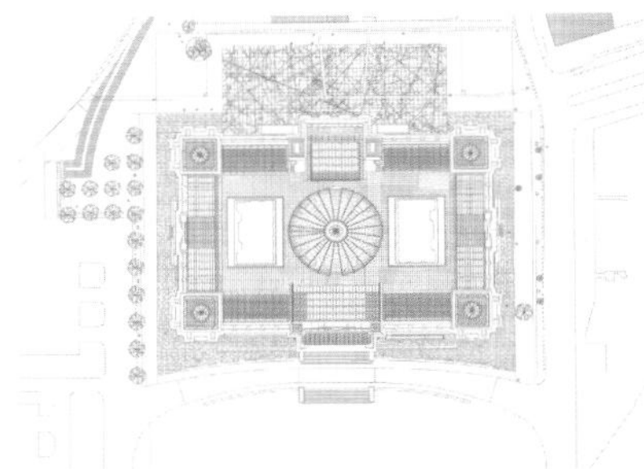

As the project developed, astonishing traces of the past and the war gradually revealed themselves (the graffiti of Soviet soldiers in 1945, the fragments of XIX-century frames, traces of masonry, and so on). The intervention sought to reconcile the new interior with the old by preserving the traces of history that resounded through the fabric of the Reichstag and allowing it to function as a living museum.

These alterations, based on environmental criteria, define new traces, not always so visible but equally telling. The new vestiges are inherent to the design of an energy-efficient building that makes extensive use of light, ventilation, and natural air-conditioning and that generates its own energy and minimizes energy and maintenance costs. Taken together, these initiatives reflect the project's germinal idea: to show that it is possible to construct "a totally sustainable public building that is responsible from the environmental point of view and virtually free of pollution."

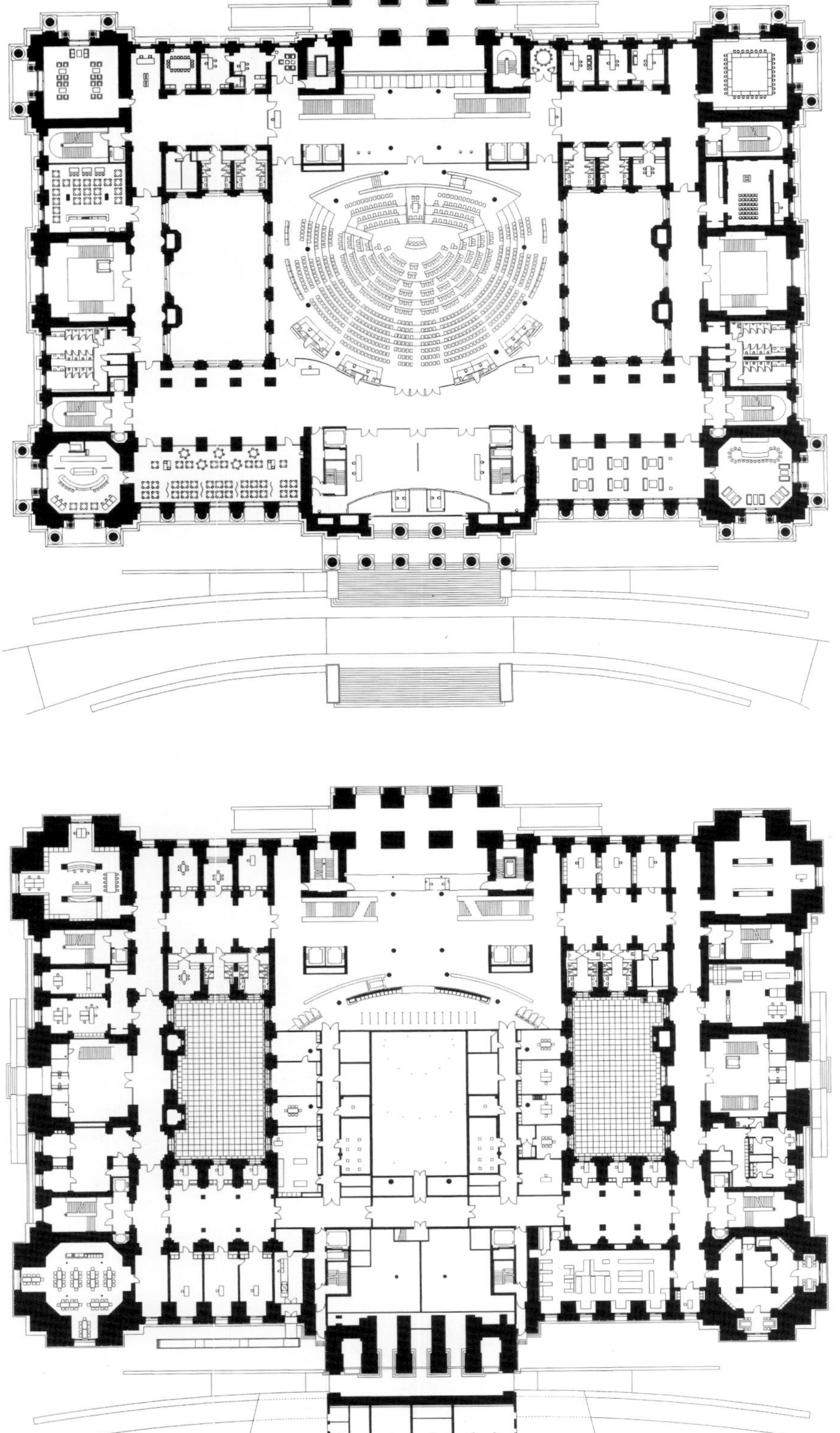

The floors of the Reichstag reveal the great functional complexity of a building designed to house the German parliament. Apart from the essential program of the building, a restaurant was housed on the top floor, as well as a press room, a bar, and a deambulatory from which people can watch parliamentary proceedings

The dome is endowed with state-of-the-art technological mechanisms: a computerized system moves the canopy so that it follows the sun's trajectory, thus avoiding the impact of direct sunlight. The "lantern" also plays a prominent aesthetic role

The dome nucleus includes a cone covered with mirrors that diffuse light and provide views of the exterior. The other mechanisms contained in this element provide natural ventilation, the exchange of heat with the exterior, and generate electricity

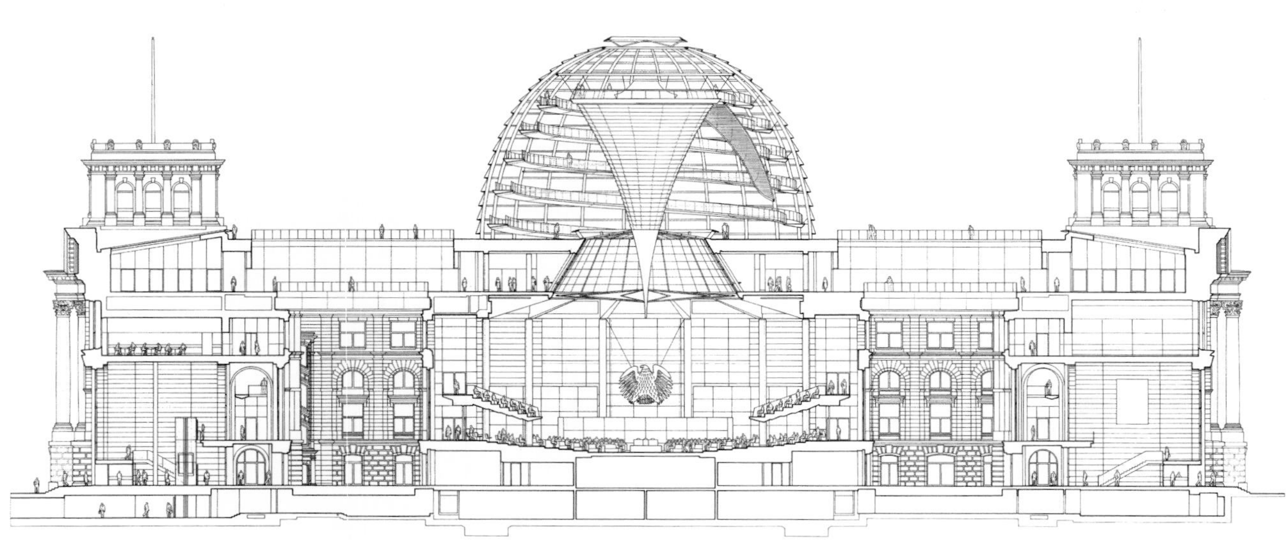

windpower energy station for expo 2000

Von Gerkan, Marg + Partners

Location: **Hannover, Germany**

Client: **Expo 2000**

Architects: **Von Gerkan, Marg + Partners**

The Dawn of the Solar Era

The future of humanity depends on whether or not it will be possible to harmonize man's coexistence with Nature via technology. This theme will be presented in a multitude of different interpretations at the Hannover World Fair. The large-scale use of solar energy might be a decisive contribution to this goal since it makes use of an inexhaustible, non-polluting natural resource.

The rising-air-current electricity power station is ideal for desert areas with a high degree of sunlight. The energy it produces can be used at home or exported. Furthermore, as inversion materials replace combustion materials, new jobs are created and non-renewable natural resources are no longer used for energy.

For the Hannover Expo, a visual demonstration model will be built of a rising-air-current electricity power station.

The station will consist basically of three parts: a tower 585 feet high and 23 feet in diameter, a turbine installed inside the tube, and a glass roof (around 60 feet in diameter), which captures heat from the sun. At the same time, in a suitable desert country (such as Morocco, Palestine or India) a real power station of 30 MW will be built to function during the Expo. With the help of the most advanced media technology, the event will therefore take place simultaneously in both places.

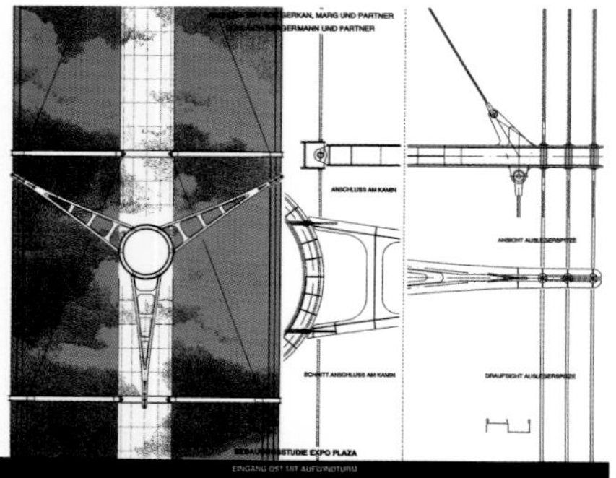

The station works using hot air, which rises since it is lighter than cold air. Thanks to the sun's rays, the air is heated beneath the huge glass roof and then rises up the tower, causing the turbine to revolve. The bigger the roof and the higher the tube, the more electricity will be produced.

This is one of the most advanced ways to exploit solar energy in terms of technology and economy. The technology is simple and available in any country. The station will be built fundamentally from concrete and glass, both common construction materials. It does not pollute the environment; neither does it consume natural resources.

The Expo 2000 rising-air-current model will not feature the real concrete tube of its desert counterpart. Rather, it will be conceived as a spectacular, innovative glass tube 585 feet high and 23 feet in diameter. Through the combination of glass and other high-tech building materials, and by applying modern building techniques, an incomparable self-supporting glass tower will be constructed. Its design separates the main forces of tension and compression. The modular glass tube will withstand the forces of compression, while a number of triangular pieces will separate the forces of tension from the building and direct them towards the ground by means of steel cables.

Since its dimensions will be too small to produce electricity economically, the turbine will not really be installed. However, visitors will be able to see how it revolves depending on the intensity of sunlight. The tube will be the visionary symbol of the Expo, the emblem of the Hannover Fair, and will remain standing after the event is over.

The rising-air-current electricity power station that will be built in the desert will consist of a huge reinforced concrete tower, and it will be the first of its kind in the world. Even so, in Spain there is a small prototype that has been successfully undergoing trials monitored by independent experts for the past seven years.

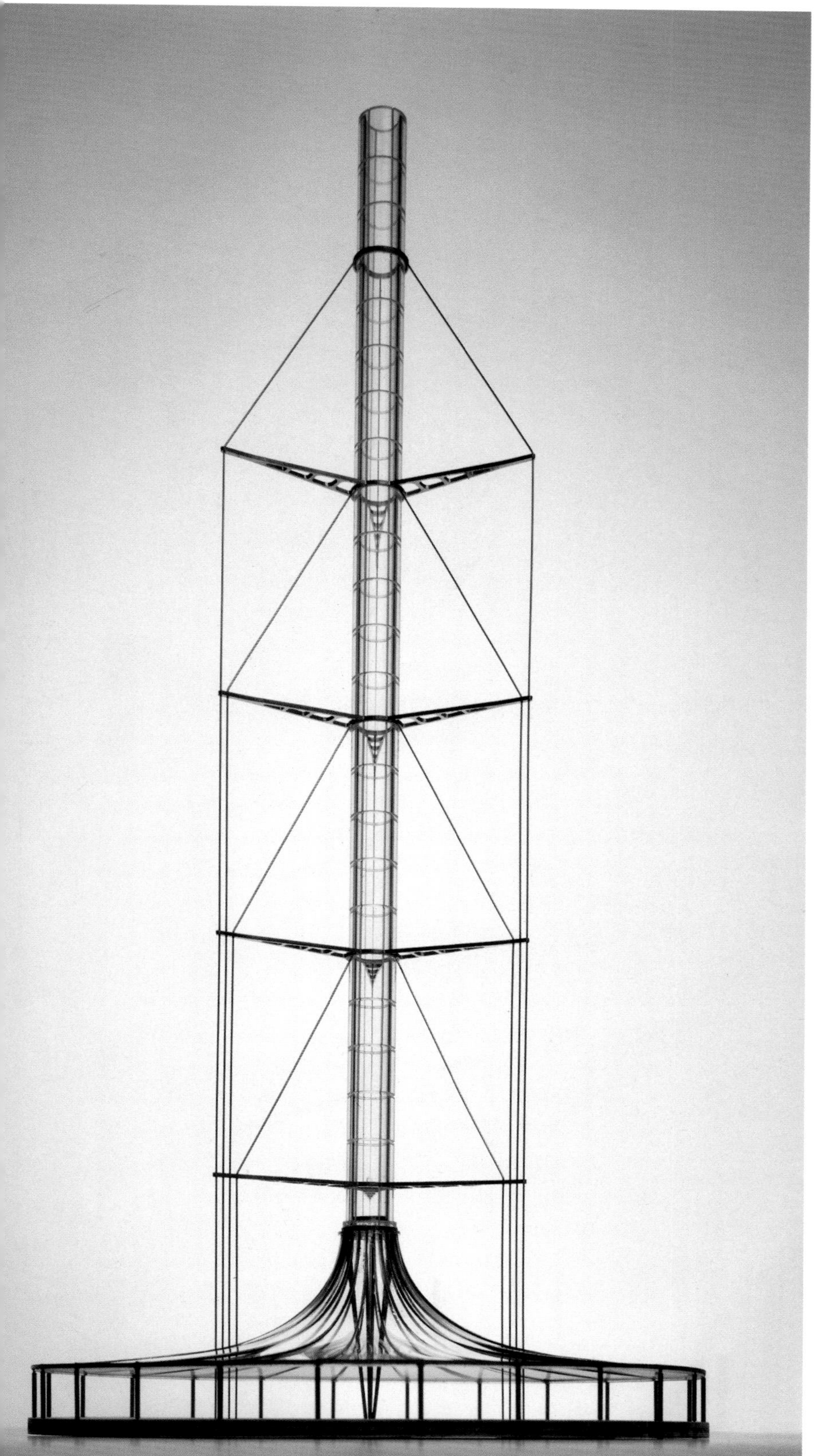

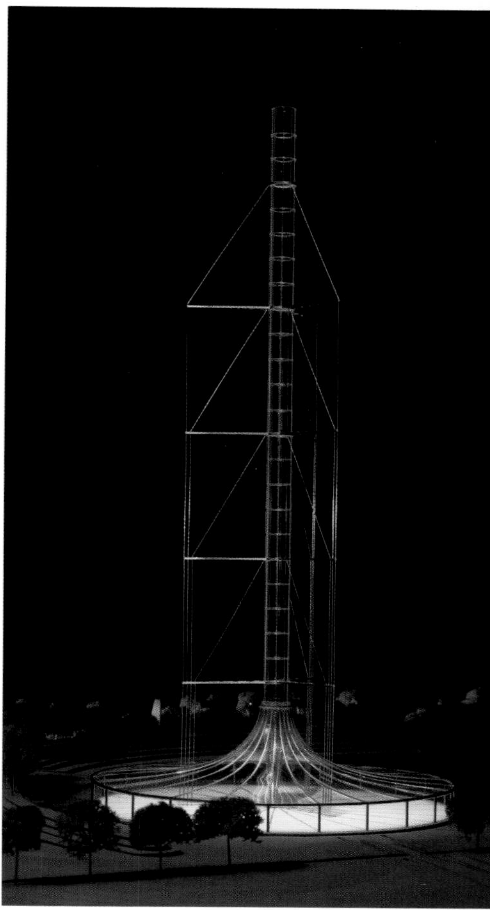

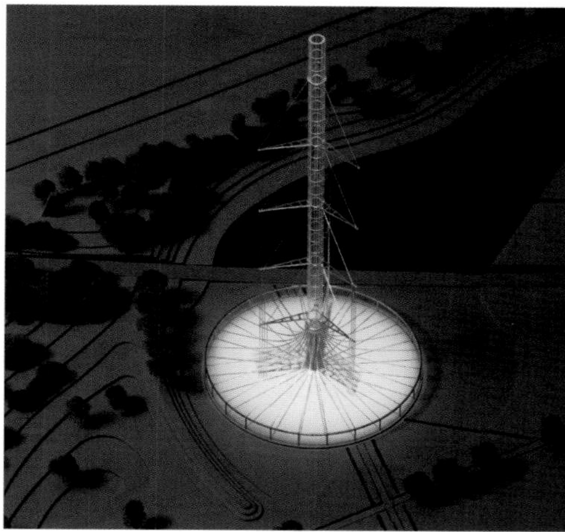

The rising-air-current power station exploits solar energy to produce great amounts of electricity. The simple technology it requires is readily available in any country

cultural center jean Marie Tjibaou in Nouméa

Renzo Piano Building Workshop

Location: **Nouméa, New Caledonia**

Client: **Development Agency for the Kanak Culture**

Construction date: **1991-1998**

Architects: **Renzo Piano Building Workshop**

Collaborators: **P. Vincent, D. Rat, A. Chaaya**

Photography: **J. Gollings, W. Vassal**

When Culture Defines Architecture

The fundamental question for the development of the Cultural Center Jean-Marie Tjibaou, in New Caledonia, was to merge its program with the creation of a symbol for the Kanak civilization that would avoid "folklore imitation, or the world of kitsch and picturesque." (1)

It´s about discovering how culture defines the required architecture. In this process, hermetic design procedures aren't used as much as open dialogue with the preexisting conditions of the place. For this, it became necessary "to try to understand how this culture was born, why it had followed certain tendencies, what philosophy had shaped it." (2)

Traditional Kanak constructions result from their osmosis with nature and are ephemeral like some of nature's materials. Their continuity is not based on their isolated longevity but on how they preserve topology and construction patterns. Another key aspect of the local culture is the concept of the landscape as an inseparable element from the architecture.

Both planes were considered during the realization of the project. In the end, the Cultural Center was placed east of Nouméa, on a small peninsula partly surrounded by sea and partly by a lagoon with lush vegetation. Similar to the Kanak settlements that aspire to be a town and a forest at the same time, the Cultural Center was conceived as a group of structures, streets, and open spaces linked by a central core of vegetation and a tree-lined walk.

Visitors gradually become familiar with the center and its activities. The access is not at the front, but through a path running parallel to the coast and the main building. The trajectory meanders upward to a promontory and ends in an elevated plaza, which is the center's main entrance.

Inside, the cultural program develops like a sort of ritual as visitors travel through exhibitions about the art, history, and religion of the Kanak civilization, as well as the island's natural spaces. The building was organized as a group of three villages to house exhibitions, open-air performances, amphitheaters, and offices.

The "villages" are made up of ten large semi-circular buildings with different purposes that, unexpectedly, open to the tree-lined walk that functions as a communication link for the center. This provides a "dramatic passage from a compressed space to an expanded one," states Renzo Piano, "From the vernacular culture, we steal its dynamics and stress points." (3) The thematic journey continues on the outside of the building where a path reconstructs the Kanak representation of human evolution and reflects on the key moments of its culture: creation, agriculture, habitat, death, and resurrection, all originated from metaphors inspired by Nature. The Cultural Center is exposed to strong winds on one side, and to mild breezes on the other. This climatic condition takes hold of the architecture, which registers the rhythms to which if is subjected. Thus, low volumes face the lagoon and windscreens face the sea to master the dominant winds and induce convection currents – the common local practice – furnishing the Cultural Center with an effective ventilation system.

Double shell structures result from the difficult task of reinterpreting the Kanak huts. Like the primitive system, wood ribs and beams support them, except these are shorter and less curved. They are clad in Iroko wood, suggesting the woven fibers of local constructions. "The outer siding strips have odd widths and spacing. The optical effect produced by the slight resulting vibration strengthens the similarity with the wind-blown vegetation." (4)

From its broader aspects to the more specific, Piano's architecture doesn't try to disappear into the local traditions, but to feed from their authenticity in order to render them universal. Ultimately, the Cultural Center is the materialization of a conscientious effort to find the critical balance between artifact and nature, tradition and technology, memory and novelty while confronting diverse rhythms like space, time, culture, and climate.

1,2,3,4 Renzo Piano Logbook. Thames and Hudson, London, 1997.

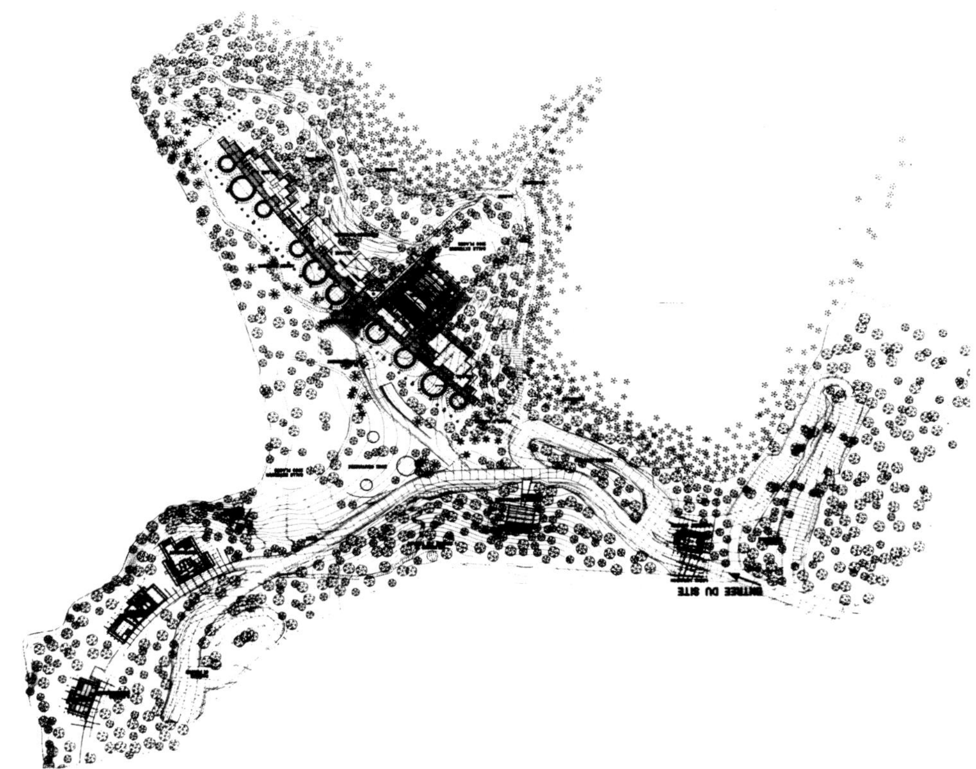
ENTREE DU SITE

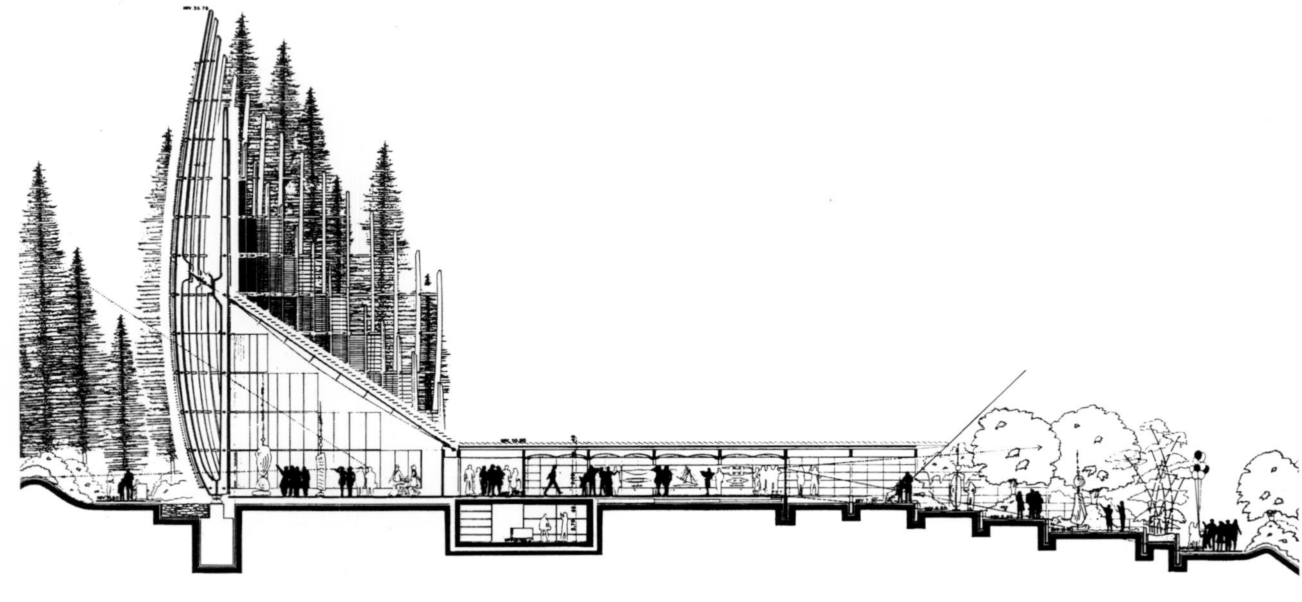

Section of the exhibition area. The first village consists of a reception area, coffe shop, exhibition halls, and a performance area

Elevation of the second village which contains a media-library and workshops

The different exhibit halls show relevant artwork from the Kanak culture.

The Iroko wood strips allow a façade configuration that permeates the light and views

Since they require very specific climatic conditions, the exhibit halls are more conventional. New technology endows the spaces with museum-specific functionality

Anchoring of the façade's structural tensors. The inclusion of the project in this book is largely due to the construction details, where the firm's technical knowledge produces excellent solutions

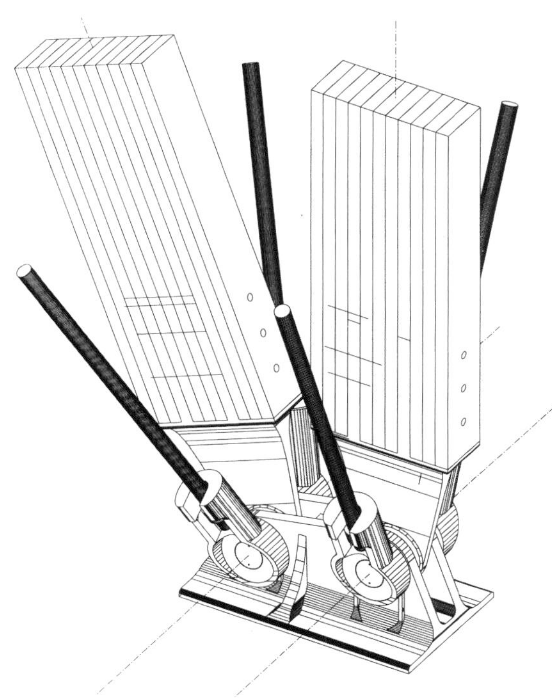

Detail of one of the exhibition halls. Iroko wood strips are also used on the interior, since they are suited to the geographic location of the project

The splendid group view can be appreciated from the sea. Renzo Piano's project finds the critical balance between artifact and nature, tradition and technology, memory and novelty

energetically efficient façades and bioclimatic roofs

energetically efficient façades and bioclimatic roofs

Tower RWE in Essen

Ingenhoven, Overdieck, Kahlen & Partner

Location: **Essen, Germany**

Client: **Hochtief AG**

Date of construction: **1994-1996**

Architects: **Ingenhoven, Overdieck, Kahlen & Partner**

Collaborators: **Achim Nagel, Klaus Frankenheim, Martin Slawic, Claudia de Bruyn, Regina Wuff**

Photography: **Christian Richters, H.G. Esch, Holger Knauf**

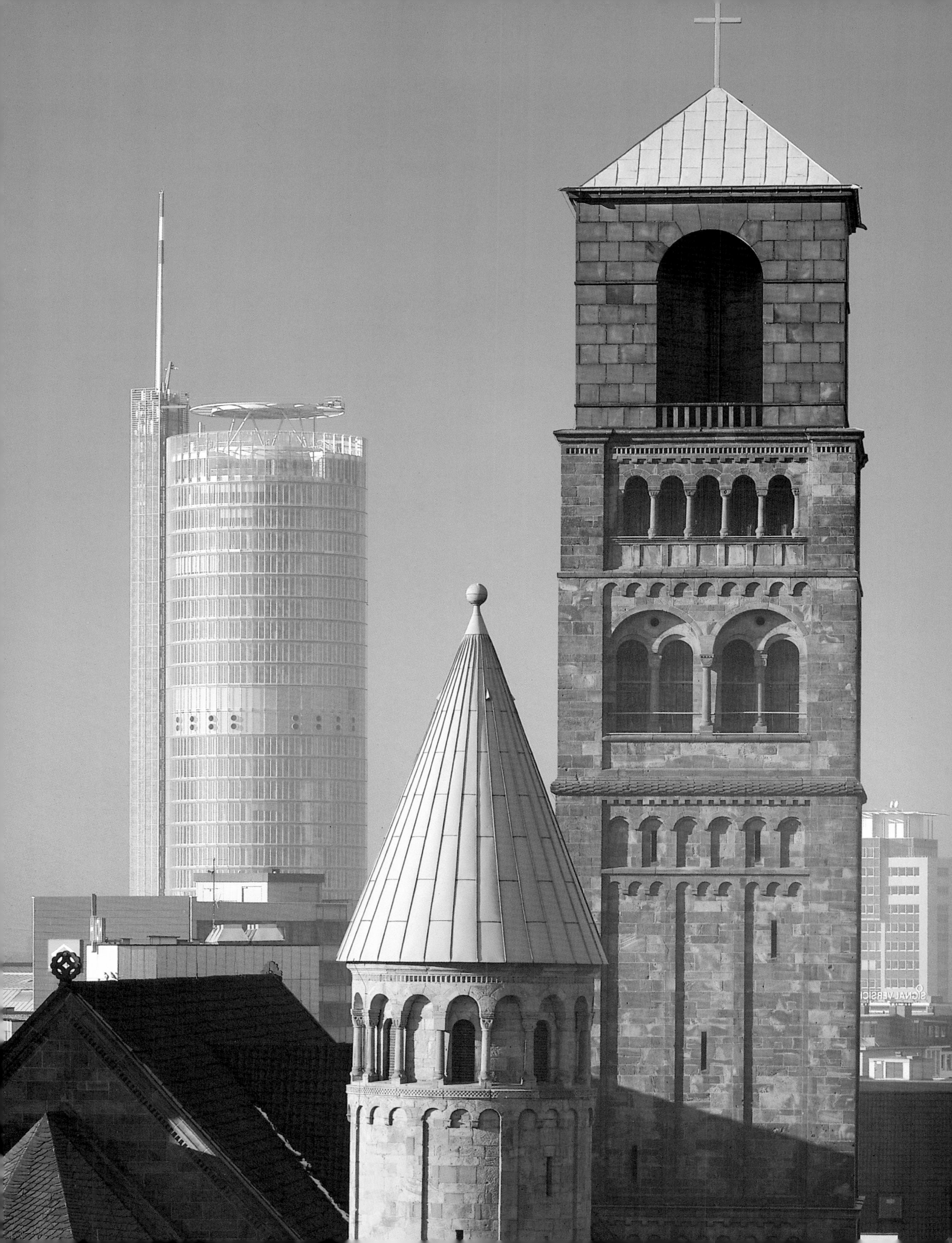

The Building's Double Façade Allows Natural Ventilation

This project is located in Essen, the geographical center of the Rhur River. The architects claim it is the first "ecological skyscraper" ever built. This 30-story circular tower, administrative headquarters for a German electric company, sits across another emblematic project – Alvar Aalto's opera building. The construction unfolds the architects' previous criteria for the Essen master plan, which included the construction of a towering Administrative Center. This space was foreseen to occupy the least possible surface of a proposed park that would connect the city center and the green belt circumventing Aalto's work.

The project's guiding principles included energy conservation and a comfortable, healthy work environment that would take into account individual user needs regarding air-conditioning, ventilation, and natural light.

This is apparent in the technical, constructional, and volumetric aspects. When compared to other prismatic forms, the cylindrical shape is ideal in terms of the relationship between exterior surface and interior volume. It also optimizes aerodynamics, energy needs, surface distribution, and choice of prefabricated elements.

The project is based on extensive studies on the optimization of controlled natural air-conditioning. In the case of cylindrical towers, one can expect air speeds that are twice the wind pressure, which eases vertical circulation of airflow and the diagonal ventilation in all stories.

Regarding the organization of space in the building, the architects chose to separate the vertical communication cores and group them into a svelte, attached column. This simplified the distribution of offices, making the most of the interior space. The office levels are configured around a nucleus; they subdivide into conference rooms, round hallways, and peripheral bands of offices and stairs that interconnect some of the levels. The outer glass skin allows natural light to reach the internal core.

The building's key characteristic is the double skin finish. This 120 meter glass cylinder marks an inflection point from the traditional American way of construction with its absolute separation between interior and exterior environments and its artificial air-conditioning. On that account, the double skin allows the RWE Tower to "breathe."

The double skin consists of an exterior sheet made of fixed glass panels – 2 x 3.6 meter modules that permit air circulation through corresponding slots – and an interior sheet with operable panels. A solar protection system is installed between both layers, which are 50 centimeters apart. Strips, placed on the setting lines for the exterior façade modules, are perforated on the right side and solid on the left side, at the lower level. The disposition is reversed on the upper level, next to the roof, which guarantees a minimum diagonal of ventilation and prevents the return of recently evacuated air back into the spaces.

The interior layer of the double skin is a conventional façade, insulated by collapsible panels that can be controlled manually. Consequently, even the upper workspaces can enjoy natural air control without having to fight wind gusts. The façade surpasses the last floor in height to protect the terrace from the wind.

The building is conceived so the users can control their own environment. However, when, the weather is forbidding, temperature is managed by an air-conditioning system with a minimum capacity of air recycling.

The RWE Tower outlines a permeable architecture and presents itself as a system of controlled exchange with the environment. Thanks to its energy and synergy efficiency, it incorporates what nature has to offer, both technically and architecturally.

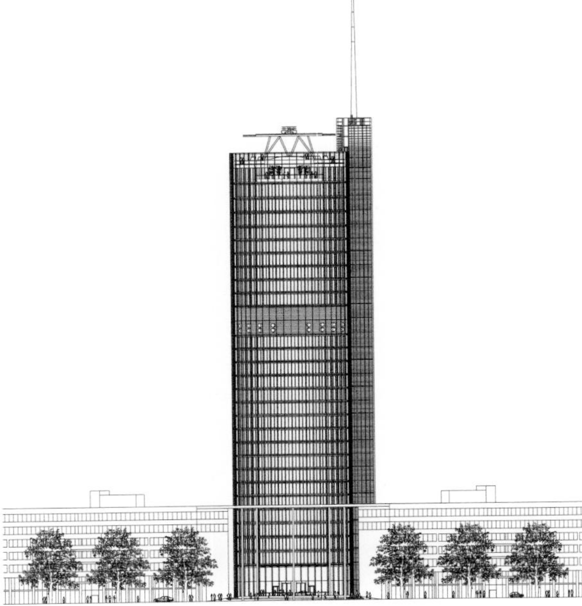

View of the elevation from Alvar Aalto's opera house

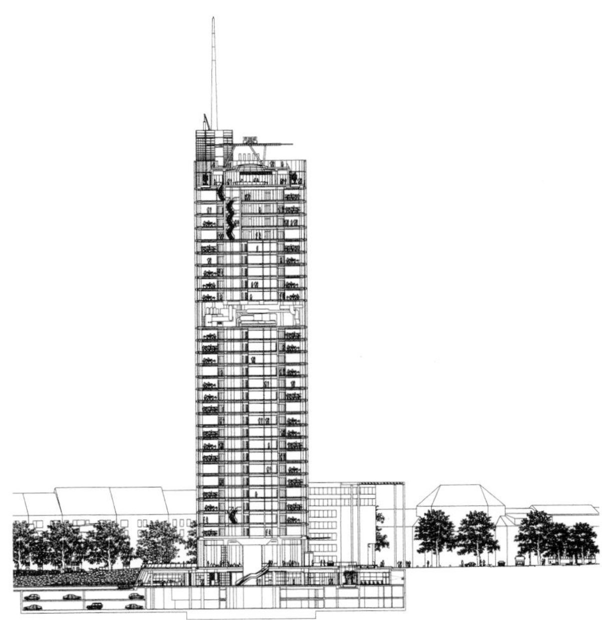

Section showing the different floors of the building

Detail of the interior with views to the city of Essen

Conference room with a skylight

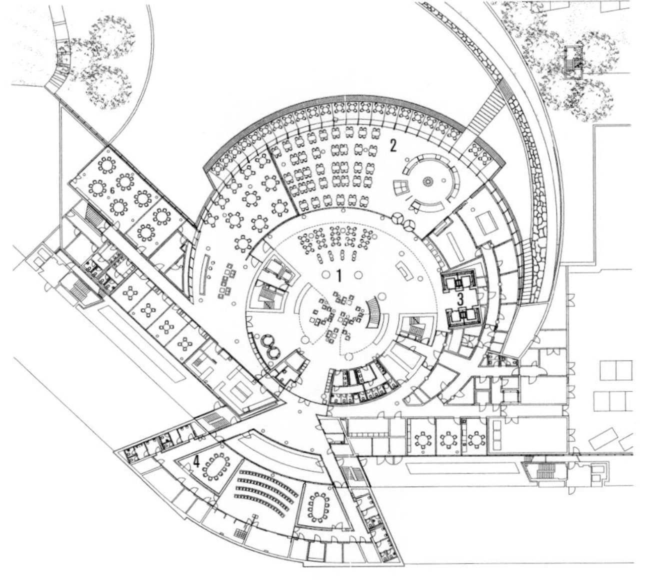

Ground floor

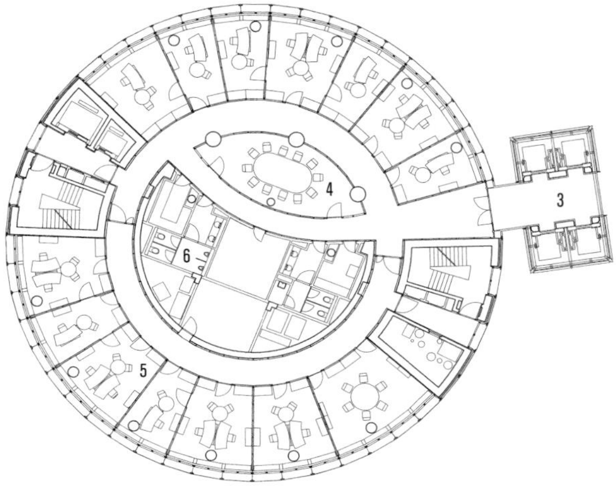

Type floor

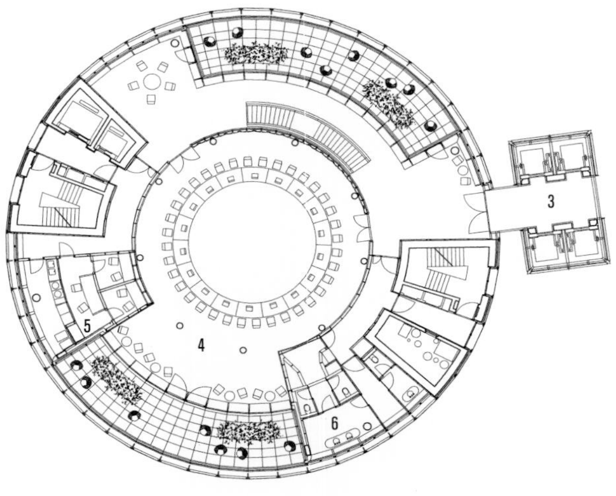

Conference room floor

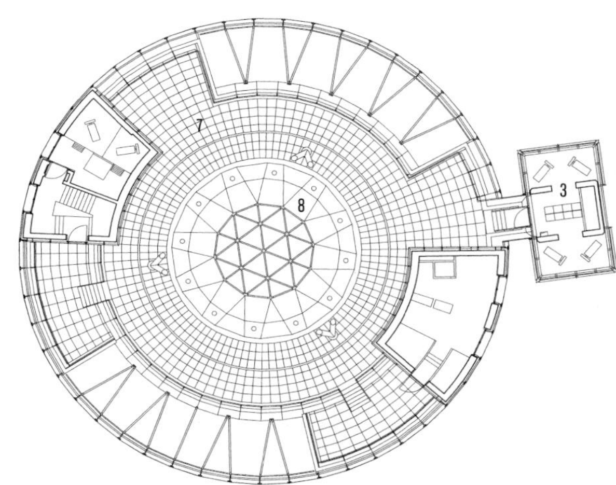

Terrace floor

1. Foyer
2. Restaurant
3. Elevator box
4. Conference room
5. Offices
6. Services
7. Terrace
8. Skylight

Next page:
Interior stairs that lead to the upper floors

Left-top picture:
View of the terrace in the upper floor

Right-top picture:
Stairs to the upper floors

Left-bottom picture:
Stairs that link the office tower and the conference room

Next page: View of the RWE company office tower.

Computerschulung GmbH
P
privat
Isenbergstraße 26

commerzbank in frankfurt

Norman Foster & Partners

Office

20-27° C

Location: Frankfurt, Germany

Client: Nervus Generalübernehmer GmbH

Construction date: 1997

Architects: Foster & Partners

Collaborators: Ove Arup & Partner, Pettersson und Ahrens

Photographs: Ian Lambot, Nigel Young

OMMERZBANK
PASSAGE
WEISS
FRAUEN
STRASSE
FRISEUR
Weißfrauenstraße
TAXI
HELVETIA
VERSICHERUNGEN

Saving Energy not As a Goal but As a Compromising Ecological Architecture

Throughout most of the year, natural ventilation can be used as a solution to maintain a pleasant climate in building interiors. If air-conditioning systems can be done without, natural ventilation and refrigeration can save energy and provide comfort.

The Frankfurt Commerzbank is based on the principle of environmental control. The project was required to include mechanisms that combine natural ventilation with protection and insulation of the building.

The building consists of a 50-story triangular tower block some 630 feet high, whose vertices are slightly rounded. The tower, complete with its podium, complements another Commerzbank building, which stands on the same site. As a whole, the intervention generates new pedestrian promenades, a public plaza and the extension of the bank foyer. It also accommodates, offices, apartments, and stores.

In order to create a less artificial and less aggressive work environment than that of a conventional skyscraper, the architects decided to tackle the problem through the façade skin and the careful distribution of spaces and the building structure.

As opposed to traditional glass towers, the Commerzbank´s point of departure was the conceptual displacement of the principle of the central nucleus. Each of the tower's three vertices has its own nucleus, which groups together elevators, stairs, ramps, and services. These nuclei constitute the bearing structure of the office units, placed every eight floors. The center of the building remains empty, forming a full-height atrium. This atrium, in turn, is subdivided every 12 floors by a glass ceiling to prevent air currents or the accumulation of smoke.

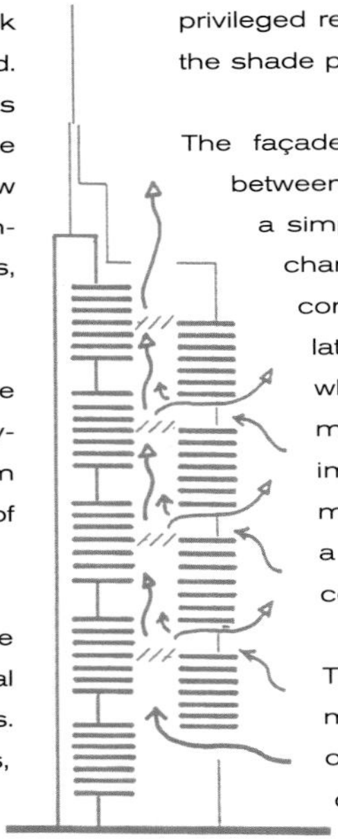

On each floor, two office zones combine with a third garden zone. Each garden occupies a height equivalent to four stories, and they are arranged in a spiral all the way up the tower. By virtue of the purifying effect of the plants, the gardens provide a high-quality microenvironment, which varies according to height and orientation. The natural ventilation of the atrium and the gardens is an integral component of the project. The arrangement of the different zones also provides natural light (from above and in diagonal) and a variety of views (to the exterior, the gardens, and the atrium).

The fact that it is possible to open the office windows overlooking the atrium means that natural ventilation may be used throughout most of the year. The same principle applies to the offices on the perimeter: the façade's triple skin establishes a privileged relationship with the exterior air that combines with the shade provided by the building.

The façade cladding system includes a ventilated cavity between a double skin of stretches of insulating glass and a simple exterior skin, which protects the building from changes in the climate. Air enters the cavity through continuous slots on the outer skin. The natural ventilation is complemented by the panels in the offices, which may be opened and closed, either manually or mechanically. When meteorological conditions impede the use of natural air-conditioning, a mechanical ventilation system is activated. In winter, a peripheral system of heating with thermostatic control is used.

The thermal conduct of the façade has also been meticulously designed in order to reduce the impact of direct sunlight, thus minimizing the need for air-conditioning and energy consumption. The fundamental principle underlying the building's design was energy economy and environmental comfort based on natural ventilation. Thanks to analysis of the façade and both physical and computer-assisted simulation, natural ventilation is provided almost all year round.

The building's prospects are optimistic and in agreement with the architects´ aims: energy saving, not as an end in itself (though it is a real objective), but as one of the essential parameters of an architecture committed to the human dimension and to the impact of human activities on the environment.

BACK-
WAREN
SAN FERNANDO
PREMIUM BANANAS
SAMSUNG

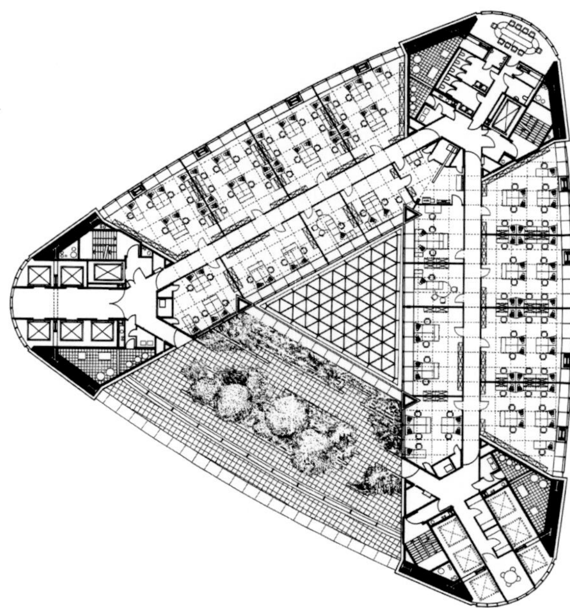

A typical tower floor. The structural and communications nuclei are at the corners of the building. Thus, the central part is left free to accommodate the atrium and the gardens. The cafeteria in one of the interior plazas enjoys natural light.

Partial section of the building, in which we observe the intersection between offices and landscaped zones. The work spaces are directly linked to these gardens, and thus enjoys natural ventilation.

Below: a general view of the building from the center of Frankfurt.

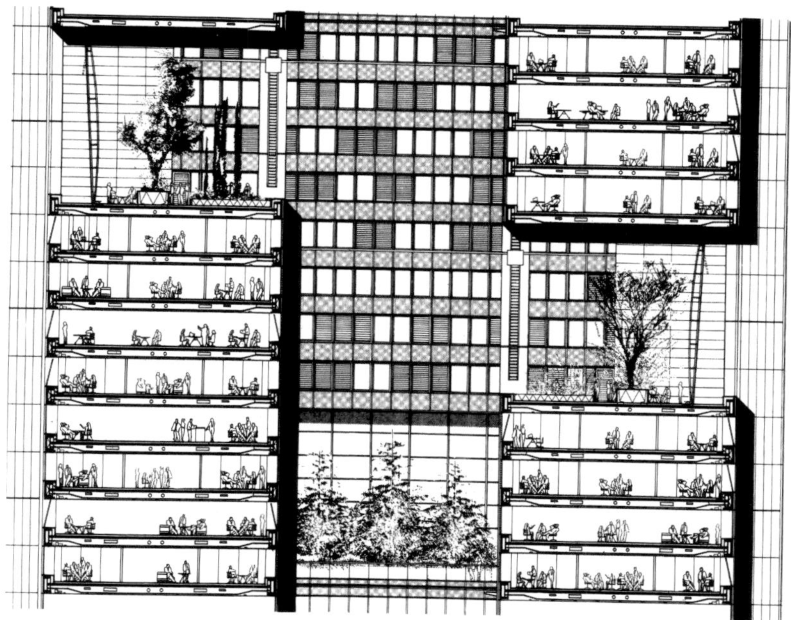

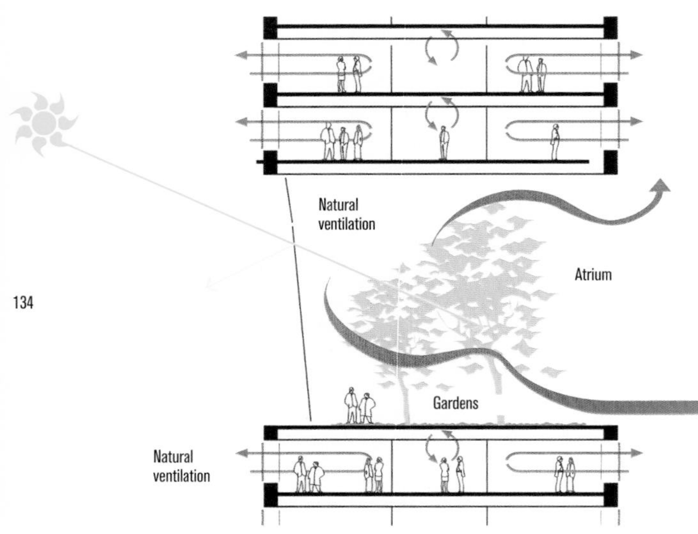

The diagram shows how the air flows through the building. The offices on the perimeter are ventilated directly from the exterior through the triple façade. The interior offices are ventilated from the gardens.

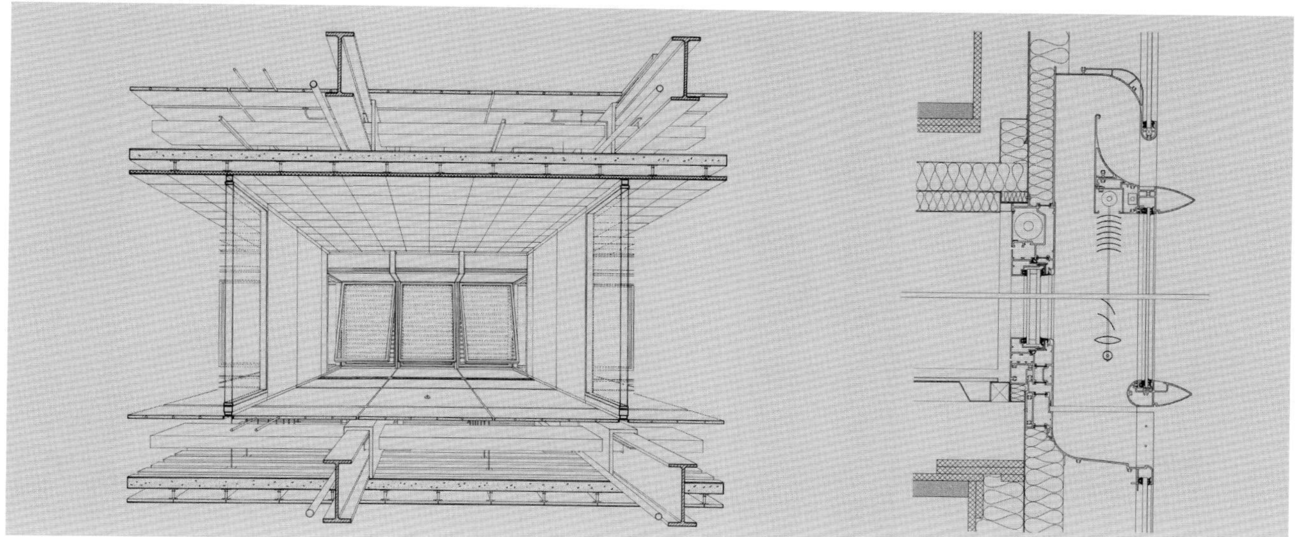

This constructional detail shows the vertical section of the double façade. The arrangement of the carpentry was designed to facilitate the penetration of air from outside without causing drafts.

Elevations of the lower floors

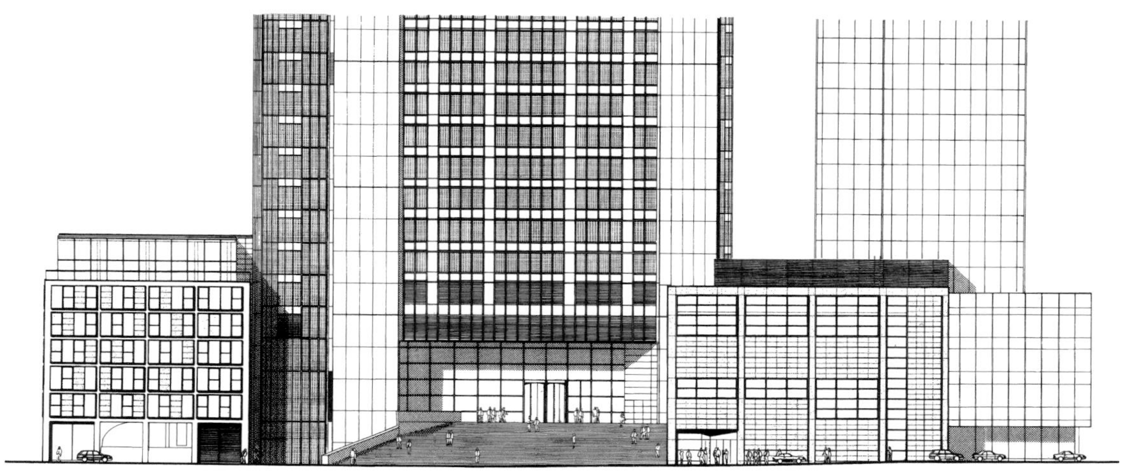

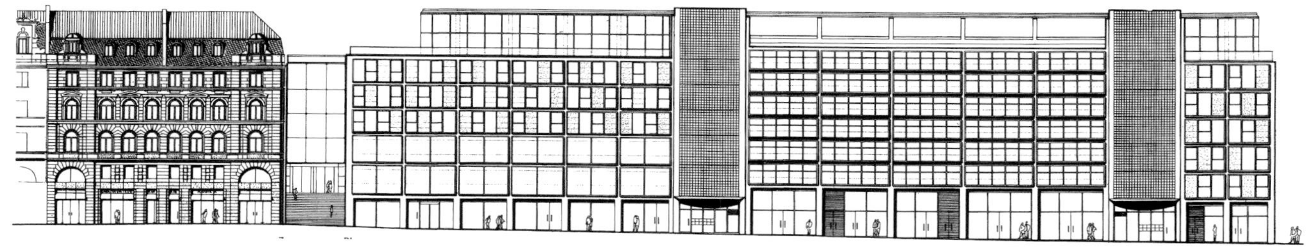

Pompeu Fabra Library in Mataró

Miquel Brullet

Location: **Mataró, Spain**

Construction date: **1997**

Architect: **Miquel Brullet**

Collaborators: **TMF S.S.**

Photographs: **Jordi Miralles**

Energy-Producing Façades

The Pompeu Fabra Library in Mataró responds to the functional program typical of public libraries. The element that characterizes and differentiates the project is the use of photovoltaic panels integrated into the façade and the roof (both 3,230 square feet), which act as constructive elements rather than mere additions.

The building incorporates a system that generates electricity and thermal energy for heating without affecting the requirements of a public library. It seeks optimum balance between energy, comfort, interior lighting, aesthetics, and economy factors.

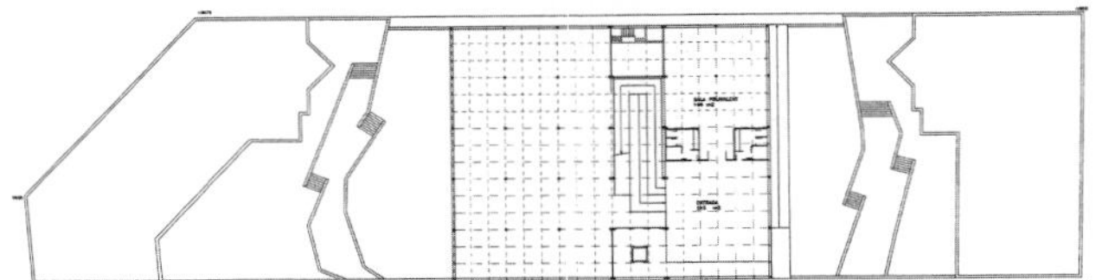

To this effect, a façade was developed based on a curtain wall with a ventilated chamber and photovoltaic cells inside. In turn, on the roof, photovoltaic modules line the slope of north-facing skylights. All this is concentrated in a unitary volume in a ground plan of approximately 100 x 120 square feet, and on three floors linked inside by a central ramp.

These hybrid modules constitute the project's major innovation: architectural elements that make it possible to close buildings opaquely or semi-transparently in a versatile way, combining aesthetics with energy production.

The system supplies part of the library's heat and electrical energy demands.

On the roof, the rows of skylights are separated from each other in such a way so as not to cast shadows. On the façade, the photovoltaic cells incorporated into the curtain wall could not be overshadowed by any cantilever structure and had to be raised ten feet above ground for safety reasons.

The skin of the façade acts as a heat absorber that protects the interior of the building, and contains a cavity in which the air is heated by direct sunlight. In summer, the air that rises upwards from the base ventilates the solar modules and prevents them from reaching extreme temperatures. In winter, the hot air is conducted to a conventional heating system either through ventilators or by free convention currents.

The multi-purpose thermal-photovoltaic module consists of photovoltaic cells with electrical connections placed between two sheets of glass. This made it possible to make opaque or semi-transparent cladding that produces electricity and hot air through exploitation of curtainwall technology.

The character of the public library's interior was determined by the photovoltaic module surfaces on the façade and the roof. The different floors receive natural light through the windows and skylights. Thanks to their design, it is also possible to regulate the interior light by means of the photovoltaic panels on the roof and façade.

The use of different photovoltaic modules was determined by the need to provide the façade with transparency, opacity or character. In turn, the building itself was modulated in terms of the dimensions of the photovoltaic panels. However, technology was only a relative conditioning factor here, and this is one of the project's most striking characteristics. The building is not clad in photovoltaic cells; rather, the photovoltaic panels are an integrated constructional element. Technology and architecture are seen here as two converging concepts, made possible by the fact that the building acts not as a mediator of technology, but as its sign.

The Mataró Library reveals how it is possible to integrate photovoltaic systems into buildings and, by doing so, to generate versatile solutions. The curtainwall appears to be the best way to integrate modules that are easy to transport and place in position.

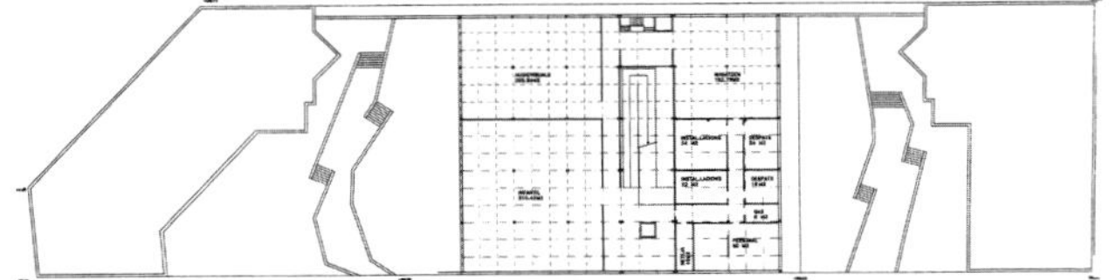

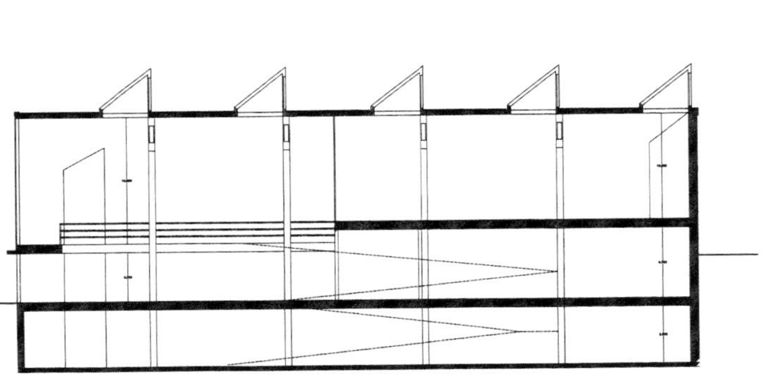

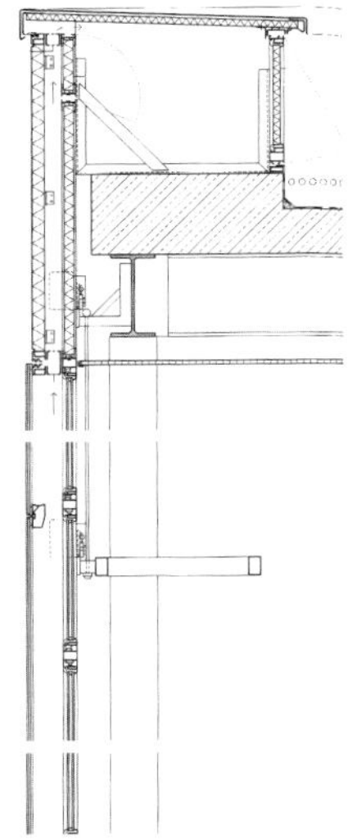

The section through the library shows the skylights arranged in four rows that make it possible for diffused light to enter from the north. Each row contains hybrid modules that constitute the project's major innovation: closing the building semi-transparently while generating electricity and hot air

The entrance to the library is a large space occupying two floors. The mechanisms used on the facade and on the skylights can be appreciated from the reception area, from which ramps provide access to the floors above

The interior spaces are generously lit, above all the common spaces: entrance, reception area, waiting rooms, corridors, and ramps. Readers can regulate the lighting in the reading room

center of overseas archives

T. Lacoste, A. Robain, C. Guieysse

Location: **Aix en Provence, France**

Client: **Overseas Archives**

Construction date: **1996**

Architects: **T. Lacoste, A. Robain, C. Guieysse**

Photographs: **Jean Marie Monthiers**

Capturing Light

Technological evolution has been a determining factor in the process of urban renewal and renovation of existing structures. What formerly appeared to be unjustifiable exercises, in many cases based on the idea of keeping up with the times in formal terms, are now fundamental operations with respect to the building's profitability and efficiency. This extension of the Center of Overseas Archives is a project committed to meeting the center's new functional demands, including environmental ones, in the light of new technologies. It also strives, through an elementary formal concept, to generate a coherent relationship between the architectures it links and the surrounding landscape.

The structure of the Center of Overseas Archives, whose purpose is to store documents related to the former French colonies, has been altered a number of times in its history. Built in 1965, it was first enlarged in 1986, when its storage capacity was doubled. Later, in 1991, its public spaces were restructured to accommodate more visitors. The result integrated the building into the urban tissue and the surrounding infrastructures. However, it is thanks to the present intervention by the French architects Lacoste, Robain, and Guieysse that this cultural complex has been endowed with a new image.

The new building stands between the silo in which the archives are stored, a large, five-story geometrical block clad with light-colored stone finely perforated on its façade. The single-story, neoclassical administrative building surrounds a paved patio. A pond with stones borders the building and isolates it toward the access façade. The pond emphasizes that the building is an object that depends on the surrounding volumes. Therefore, the building acts as a neutral backdrop while providing a splash of color among the neat arrangement of green chestnut trees in the parking lot.

Besides establishing a formal link within the complex by virtue of its minimalist image, the building captures energy. It is a geometrical extension placed at right angles to the two original volumes and acts as a screen against the winds that blow from different directions depending on the time of year or day. The essential characteristic of the building's cladding is a skin of red-ocher mortar finely applied to 4 x 8-foot modules that completely cover the volume. These modules open alternatively to the exterior in the form of folds, in response to the wind and sunlight at different times of the day and year. The interior is lit mainly from above by means of 14 trapezoidal light shafts that complement the side folds. The cladding also acts as a soundproofing and heat-insulating agent that maintains a constant temperature.

Once inside the building, we find austere geometrical spaces where light takes center stage and floods everything in a controlled way. Contrasts are established between the access foyer and the exhibition hall on the ground floor, the reading room on the floor above, and the administrative offices in the existing building. The main reason for this expansion is the reading room, a space of simple lines that occupies the entire first floor of the project. This totally bare room contains no visual distractions; its walls and ceiling are paneled in light-colored wood, and the floor is covered with parquet. In the center of the room are four large wooden tables. Presidential stalls and booths stand on one side and tables for specific consultations, such as large-format documents and maps, can be found on the other side. No direct

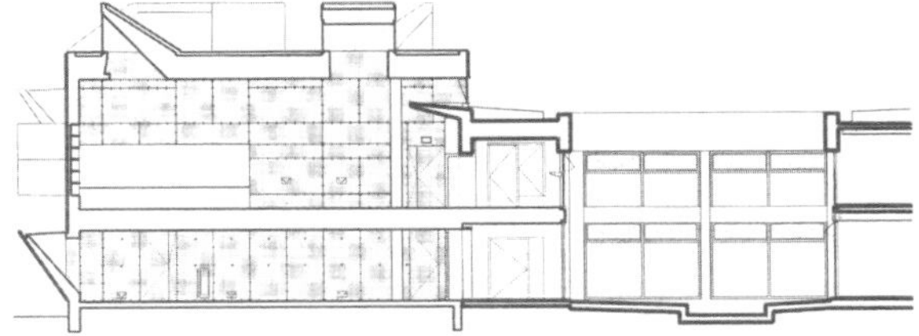

light enters the room, which is illuminated from the openings in the roof and the façade. The folding panels on the exterior perform two fundamental functions: they act as reflectors to diminish light penetration inside and as sun traps to supplement the internal heating system.

This project endows the Center of Overseas Archives with a new image, thanks to the technology and materials employed. A solid, striking volume, it also respects the surrounding architecture and landscape, with which it establishes a harmonious dialogue.

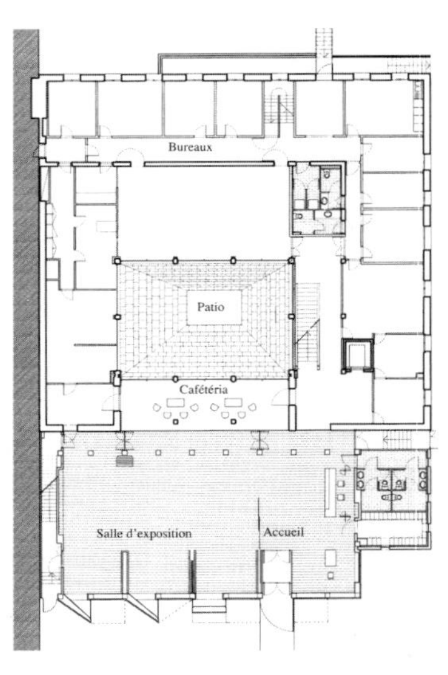
Bureaux
Patio
Cafétéria
Salle d'exposition
Accueil

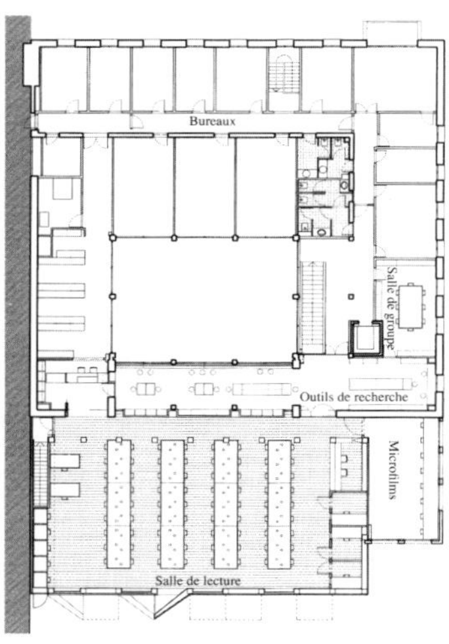
Bureaux
Salle de groupe
Outils de recherche
Microfilms
Salle de lecture

The project by these young French architects consists of a solid volume containing a system of openings on the roof and the façade that relate it to its surroundings. The lighting system for the reading room was studied down to the last detail, to protect readers from the glare of direct light.

Bordeaux-Mérignac Air-Traffic Control Center

Bertrand Bonnier

Location: **Bordeaux, France**

Client: **The French Air Base Department**

Construction date: **1996**

Architect: **Bertrand Bonnier**

Collaborator: **Laurent Joannel**

Photographs: **Hervé Abbadie**

Aerial Plantation

One of the greatest challenges contemporary architecture must face is to establish a dialogue between building and technology. Today, rather than exploiting technological advances to apply them to construction systems, architecture itself is conceived as a technological product on the basis of its spatial organization, specialized environments and designed forms. Furthermore, when the program itself includes high technology elements and systems, the architect must accommodate them and design refreshing, innovative forms. The direct, descriptive, and representative forms of the architectural idiom have been transformed into more oblique, allusive and indirect figures.

Architect Bertrand Bonnier won the competition for the new air-traffic control headquarters (CESNAC) at the Bordeaux-Mérignac airport. His design is a clear, schematic example of the aforementioned complex relations, the very contradictions of which often enter into mutual conflict. The program posed a fundamental, complicated design problem. The challenge lay in creating an ideal space in which to house highly precise activities and delicate instruments, in a stringent, orderly fashion. The building performs a major strategic function as provider of national air traffic information for approximately fifty airports and numerous control posts in France. The fact that the center acts as the brains behind French air-traffic control procedures attracted the latest high-tech trends in scientific and technological research to both the interior and exterior of the project. Moreover, the architect was required to meet an additional challenge: to integrate the object into its surroundings, a chaotic jumble of airport installations, while reflecting its function and the activities it accommodates.

The volume responds radically and, in a way, contradictorily, to the requirement's complex relationships. It consists of a huge sloping roof almost entrenched into the ground that emerges gradually like a great flagstone that shelters the center's different activities. In order to give visual expression to the idea of ground, rather than to that of an aircraft taking off, shrubs were planted on the roof like a large hanging garden, which camouflages the building by simulating a slope in the landscape. At the same time, it acts as an excellent soundproofing element. The heaviness of the roof contrasts with the lightness of the glass façades and the aerodynamic lines of the ventilation control instruments that are installed in the middle of the roof. These sheltering wings, an ambiguous metaphor, protect the huge computers in perfectly air-conditioned rooms divided into two bodies linked by the interior patio. This patio contains the main entrance and the stairs that provide access to the offices.

The lower part of the volume contains the calculation areas and technical installations. The higher part, split into three levels, includes the offices and the administrative area. This part of the building, oriented toward the setting sun, is clad with perforated timber panels fastened to a steel structure and slightly separated from the façade. The building's metallic sections and prefabricated elements both follow simple design lines.

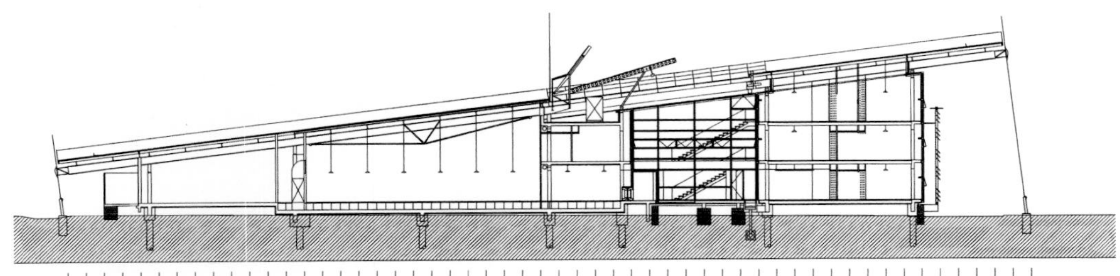

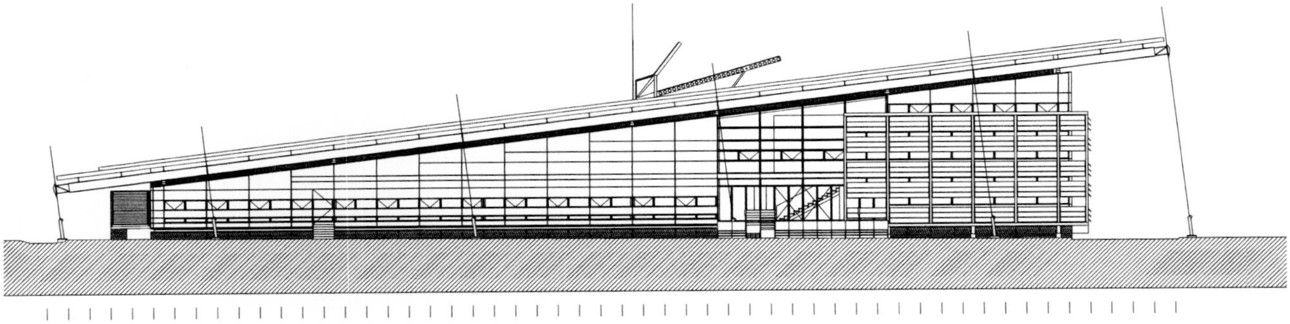

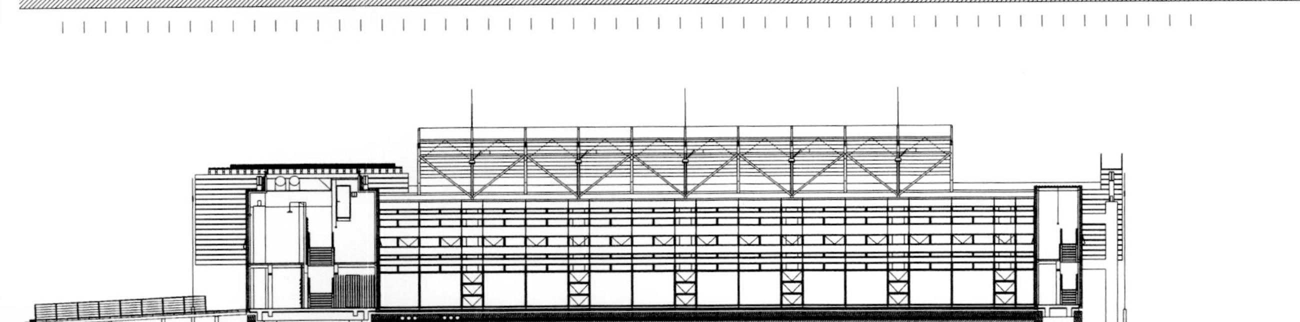

Both the section and the elevation clearly show how the roof slopes roof over the rooms of the French Center of Navigation and the Air-Traffic Control Department. "It is a huge plant ceiling that protects the French sky"

The highly protected installation between earth and sky provides insulation and comfort. The architecture, though technical, is rustic in the landscape sense, since it incorporates plant mechanisms that convert it into a sophisticated, "rural" building

The building breathes on its perimeter and also through an open interior patio that includes vegetation. The façade consists of several layers to guarantee protection from direct sunlight and effective natural ventilation

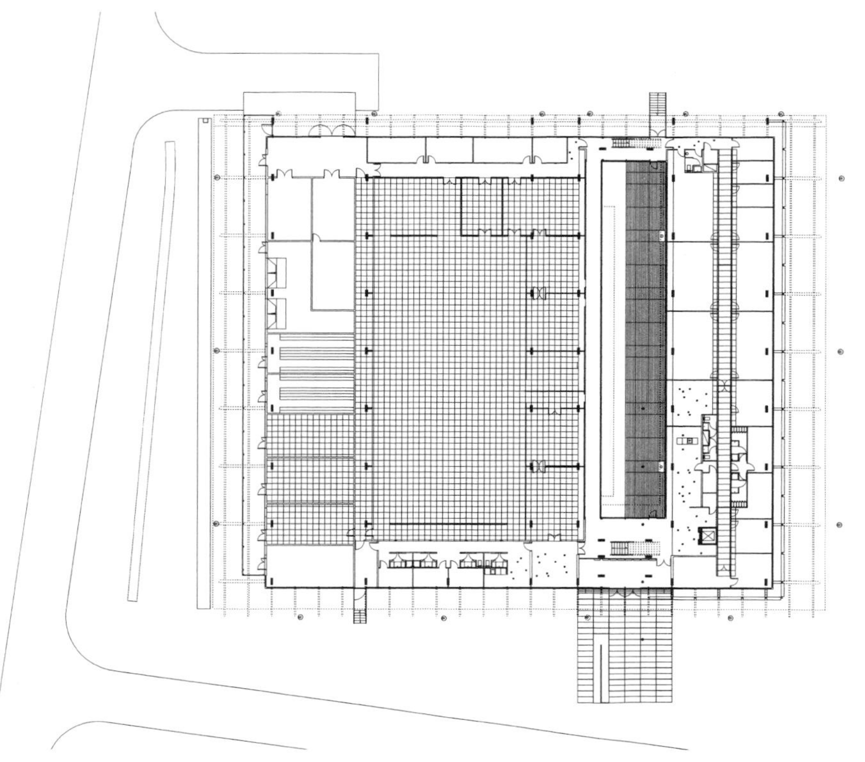

new millenium ecological arch

new millenium ecol

new millenium ecological architecture

new millenium ecologic

cological architectu

new millenium ecolog

millenium ecological archite

new millenium ecological architectu

the evolution of

ew millenium ecologic

new millenium ecological arc

new millenium ecological

new millenium ecological architecture

nium ecological archite

enium ecological arc

millenium ecological archit

new millenium ecological architec

ew millenium ecological ar

new mi

new millenium ecologi

new millenium ecological archit

new millenium eco

millenium ecological architecture

new millenium eco

new millenium ecological ar

architecture

New millenium ecological architecture

water purifier in Amiens

Edouard François

Location: **Amiens, France**

Client: **Town Hall of Amiens**

Architects: **Edouard François and Le K Associés**

Collaborators: **Nathalie Leroy, Clément Willemin, John Aubert**

Subtle Transparency in the Landscape

Edouard François' project for the Amiens water purifier is a unique example of this kind of infrastructure. The program of a water purifying plant, whose purpose is to treat contaminated waters and then return them to their original courses, already contains a high ecological content. Nonetheless, these kinds of buildings are generally linked to areas of heavy industry that are inaccessible to casual visitors. They tend to be architectural objects that have little to do with the landscape, yet are directly related to their industrial surroundings. This project's unique quality is the way in which François has managed to make the purifier and these relationships enter into a harmonious dialogue. The site is unusual because there is no point of built reference and the nearest person is 500 yards away. For once, the site's qualities match its program: natural surroundings set aside for an infrastructure whose purpose is ecological. The guiding principle of the architectural project is to adapt the plant to its context, so that it does not intrude upon the landscape in any way. Furthermore, in terms of accessibility, it is not common for a water purifying plant to invite visitor into the natural landscape and have them "participate" in the Complex.

The main link between architecture and the environment is established through the landscaping project. The site is a wide-open space, half natural and half agricultural, a vast landscape consisting of woods and marshes. The built part of the project stands exactly on the border between the agricultural area and the wetlands, on the slope of a hill. The presence of reservoirs on the bank's slope supplies an element that responds to the built volumes through an interposed landscape.

The limestone excavations on the slope are made of undulating plinths, bases for groves of trees, greenhouses and flowers. The green masses, either vegetation or built, form a chain along the site. The buildings and Nature form a whole that is visible and identifiable as a new, sensual and colorful artificial landscape. The site, like a landscape of contrasts between Nature and human intervention, is presented as a wide, pedagogical and ecological collection, not as a catalogue of trees. The plant is located near the riverbank, halfway between the fields and the wetlands, in order to be as hidden as possible. From the road higher up, the volumes disappear on the slope. From the path below, designed as a promenade, the existing woods disguise the façades. In this way, a balanced relationship with the landscape is established.

The skin of the construction is light, rot-proof timber latticework, an all-enveloping natural veil that is as mysterious as silken cloth. It allows the visitor to perceive what it covers: concrete, inevitably used as the strong material for the reservoir's shells and the technical buildings. Wide panoramas that open onto the landscape break these façades. This transparency is emphasized by an abundance of light that illuminates the interior through supports of colored, serigraphed glass, which transmit messages to the visitors. Huge slides are projected to explain the functions of the complex; there will also be moving photographs on the landscape.

From the air, one can see four strictly aligned, homogeneous boxes and, further up, another isolated box for the water services. They all have the same dimensions, the same deep anchoring in the ground and the same latticework skin. As a result, the project combines the landscape's natural elements with the requirements of a program that, at first sight, may seem incompatible with a public park. This is the culmination of an interactive process between man and structure.

Computer simulations that show the interior of the purifying plant. The façade is a wooden veil that conceals the concrete behind and lessens the impact on a landscape hitherto devoid of buildings

The inner itineraries have been carefully designed to make the visit to the plant both instructive and entertaining. Slide projections on the walls and the separation between pedestrian and vehicle paths allow visitors to admire the plant without having to avoid tankers<

Hortus sanitatis

Njiric + Njiric

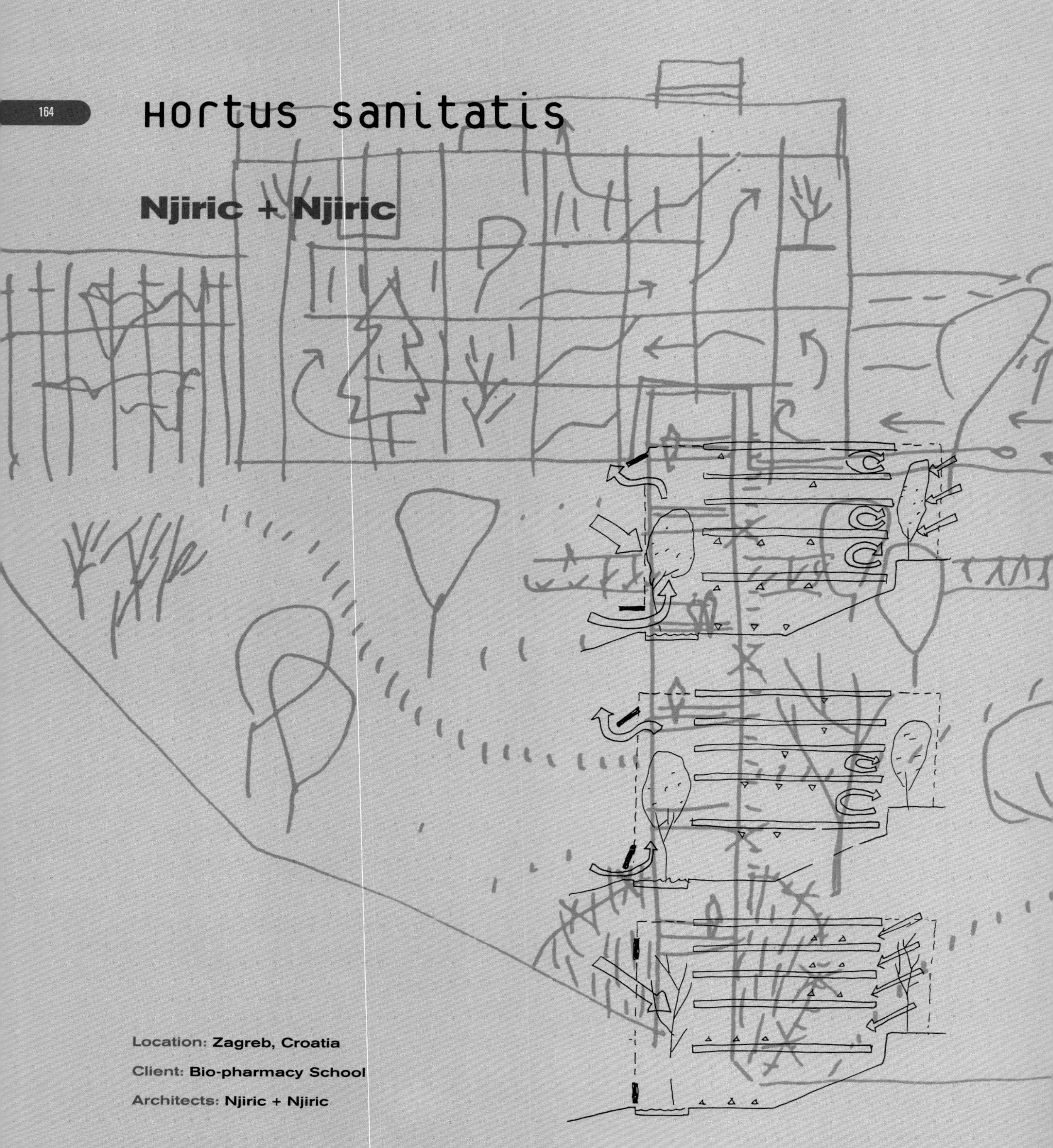

Location: **Zagreb, Croatia**

Client: **Bio-pharmacy School**

Architects: **Njiric + Njiric**

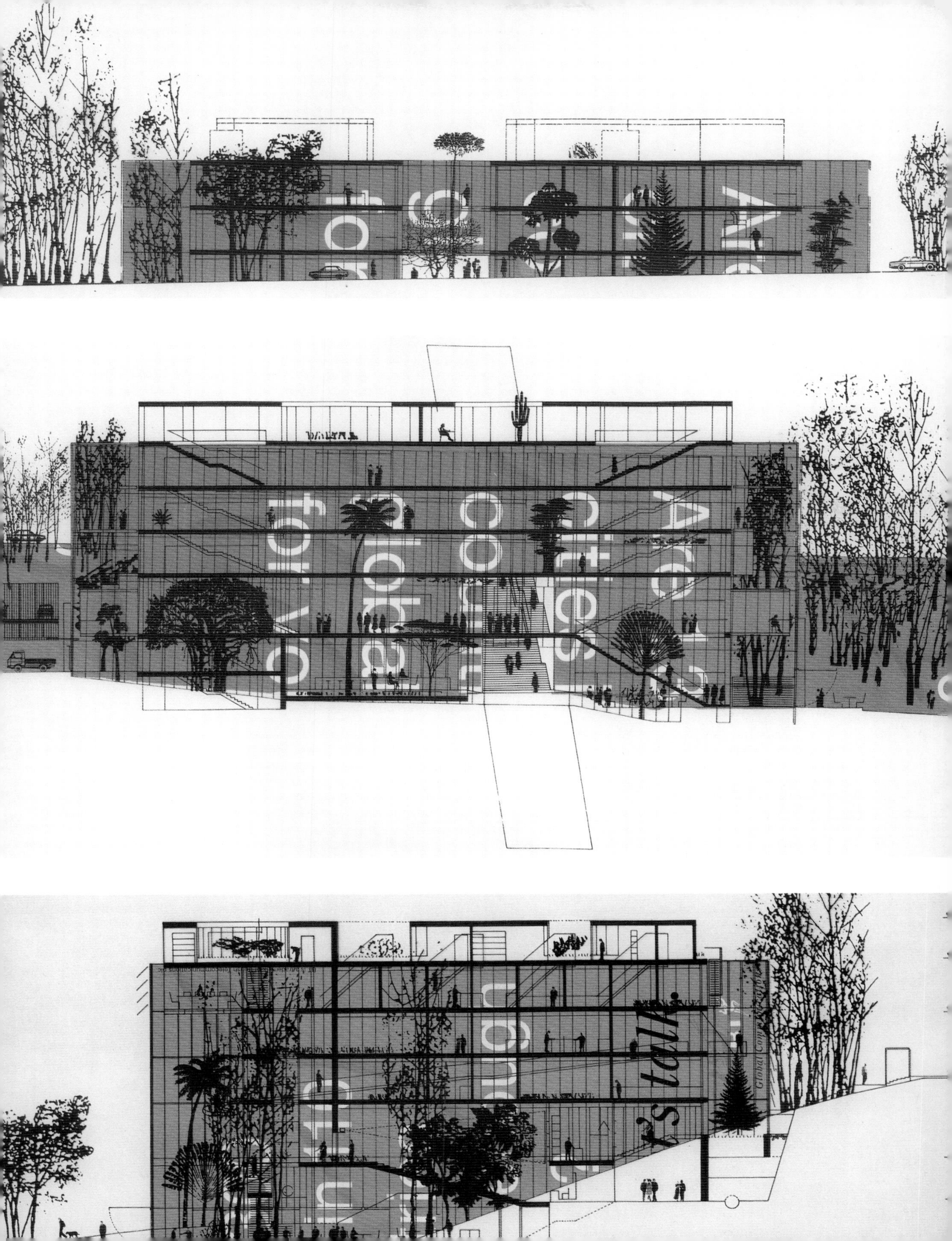

A Compressed Landscape

One of the requirements of the new School of Bio-Pharmacy was to gather the different programs dispersed around the city of Zagreb. The school owned the Botanical Gardens, so the last adjacent lot was offered to them for their new buildings. Njiric + Njiric emerged as the only firm that dared to build on the gardens.

The location is a typical row lot, alongside a neo-baroque axis. This location influenced the project with various urban-context issues.

The Hortus Sanitatis is like a constricted landscape. A core, or structural hardware, supports a low-budget, low technology conservatory, as if it were a software extension. Additional classrooms, ramps, staircases, and homeopathic and anthroposophic "artifacts" complement it. An intermediate zone performs a gradual transition towards the landscape.

A vegetation filter becomes a second skin for the façade and is articulated according to the building's orientation. Continental vegetation is used on the south side, perennials on the north, and Mediterranean varieties on the west.

The connecting paths are diverse: the shorter one is for daily use and is more comfortable for teachers and students; the "Bellevue" route is for visitors; the homeopathic path crosses the gardens with suspended greenery and the public road

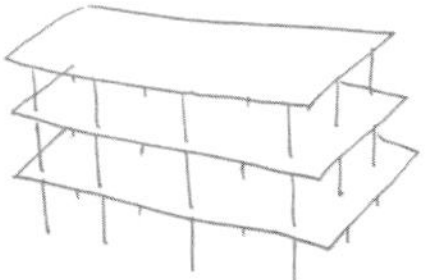

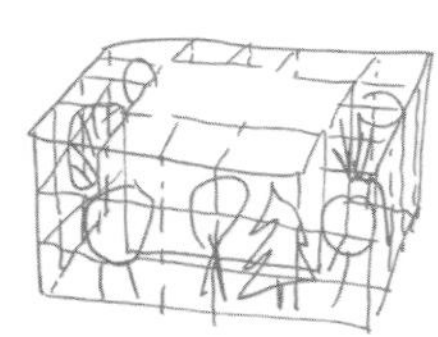

opens an urban passage into the building. The architects believe that an artifact doesn't necessarily have to be integrated into the landscape. It should, however, be well planned and compact enough to leave as much of the area as untouched as possible. Quite a few of their projects deal with congestion; be it structural (Baumaxx), a condensed landscape (Hortus Sanitatis), or a series of localized concentrations (Glasgow Cloisters).

Their method consists of a series of deductions in an effort to capture the essential idea, on any situational or architectural scale, that can be applied and developed further.

Their architecture is telegraphic. Their sketches are ideograms. At times, the idea appears like a sudden "explosion," and at other times, it occurs near the end, like with

Hortus Sanitatis. On many sites, they just remove the substance and concoct the ingredients or condense the scheme, striving all along for the minimum expression, a kind of free-style minimalism.

Yet, their idea of synthesis doesn't relate only to the notion of invention. They ask themselves if they always have to invent anew, or if they should just improve things and bring existing situations up to date. They question if a specific place really needs "Architecture." The new building for the School of Bio-pharmacy reflects a sort of concentrated landscape, a logical, internalized extension of the nearby botanical garden. It extends over the park and is traversed by an urban landscape.

Here, the building is contemplated neither as an integrated element or a disassociated one. On the contrary, just like their icons, half way from the originating idea, their architecture is understood like a catalyst within a landscape piece.

Their economy of resources and the readability of their immediate language, almost ad-like, could be associated to their perceptions: "More than ever, architecture and urban planning have more to do with productivity, free-market laws, and the real economy. All that counts is the logistics." Another explanation is that, "In this free-for-all Balkans, with constant changes, premeditated actions, emotional escape, and great levity, there is no room for mistakes in approach."

1,2,3,4 Njiric + Njiric, interview with Yoros Simeoforidis. Quaderns, Issue 219.

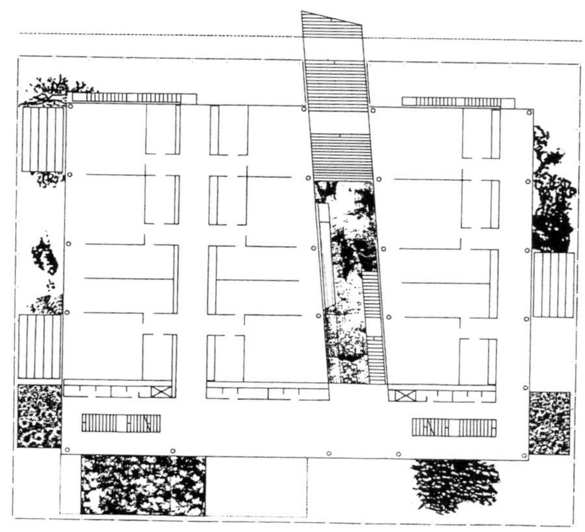

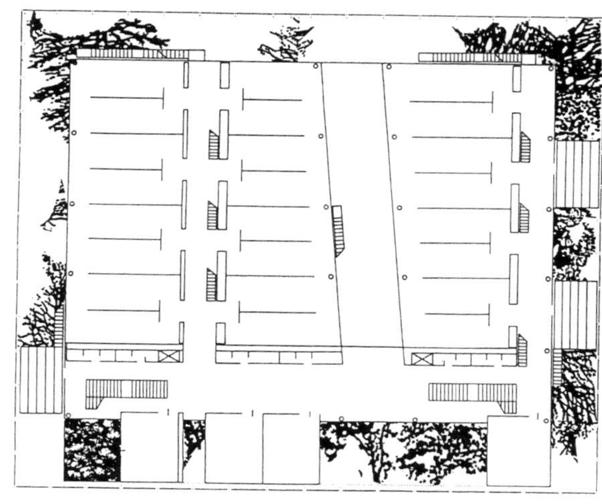

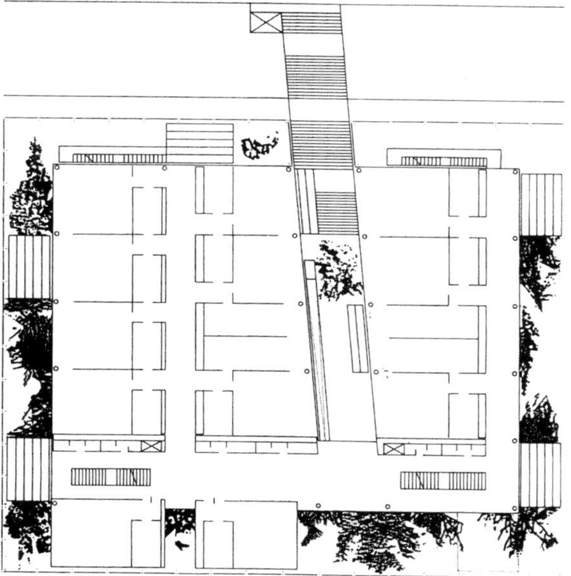

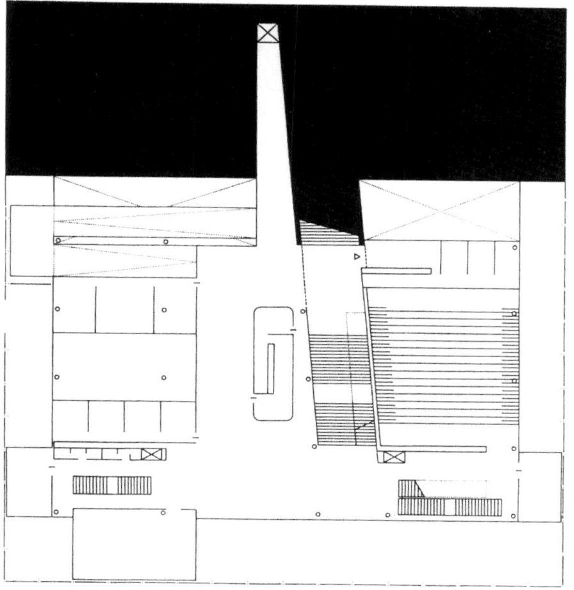

The program for the Bio-pharmacy School project congregates the departments that were dispersed all over the city. The building is conceived as a complex shelter for functional programs, open spaces, and gardens. The plans show an organized structure, with multiple, interconnecting paths

Hector Petersen Museum

Roche, DSV & Sie. P

Location: Soweto, South Africa

Architects: Roche, DSV & Sie. P

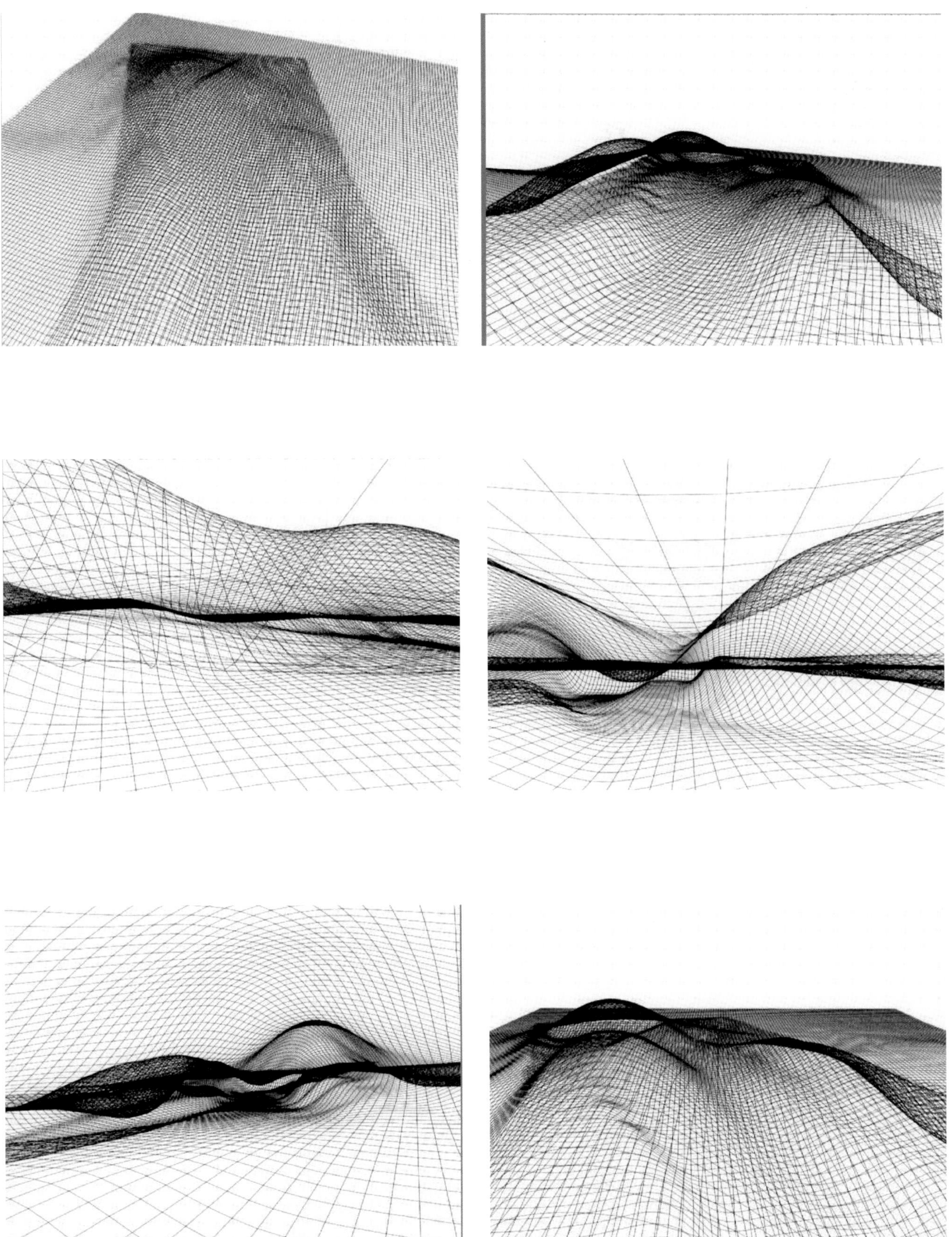

The Media is the Landscape

The projects of R, DSV & Sie strive to become an essential part of their site, suggesting an "in situ attitude" rather than provocation or departure. Their strategy is "make do with less." Their previous projects have evoked an existing vacuum (Maïdo, The Reunion, 1997), redirected an artifact in relation to the environment (Sarcelles, France, 1994), and established a common understanding between house and trees (Compiége, Saint Saveur, France, 1994). For a long time, they were looking for an instrument that would enable them "to explore the minimal act, somewhere between the not-much and the just-enough, where the territorial change stemming from architecture would be steeped in prior geographies, where the development can work its way in, and embed itself in what it was supposed to dominate, to exacerbate issues of mutation and identity."

Likewise, within this demonstration of a processing economy, it wasn't enough to contrast the already existing site with its future, in an encounter between the image of the exposed context and the image (in photomontage) that embraces the architectural project. They wanted a media that would allow them to grasp the process in the breakdown of successive hypotheses, something that would show the scenario of contaminated geography, when the structure becomes impregnated with the site.

Projects like Hector Peterson Memorial (Soweto, 1997) and Acqua Alta (Venice, 1998) illustrate this idea.

Both of these projects have a seemingly classic point of departure. The first case entailed the realization of a museum-memorial in Soweto – 2,000 square meters for exhibition halls, archives, and conference rooms. The second project involved remodeling a 4,000 square meter mall, located in the port of Venice, including an auditorium, bookstore, amphitheater, restaurant, and a gallery.

The designs of these projects resulted from morphing and its variations. Morphing lies at the root of a software program that "makes it possible to merge image A with image B by means of a topological shift of salient dots. With the "Warp" technique, which is a variant of this process, it is possible to produce this alteration, but without being aware of the resulting B. Image A can thus be easily manipulated, and distorted, when it comes into contact with a program and a scenario, but it cannot sidestep its own matter, its own physicality, by resisting it."

The morphing software calls for "a body, a generic physical matrix. There cannot be a blank page or an empty screen. The skin of the photographic, cartographic image is transformed and metamorphosed in one and the same envelope (Acqua Alta in Venice), in one and the same matter (Lava in Sainte-Rose, Tavé Foundation), and it undergoes manipulations akin to folding (Soweto), extrusion and scarification."

In Soweto, the landscape folds in on itself and the architectural fragments adjust themselves to the new topography. In Venice, the relationship between site and architecture becomes more intense than in Soweto. In this project, we witness a sort of submission of the architectonic object. It is "forced out of the real, to question our own perception." Nothing seems more pertinent to the architects than "an architecture that straddles such ambiguities."

The Soweto and Venice projects emerge from Roche's "amorphism" concept: "The project is no longer the issue of an abstract projection, but of a distortion of the real."

It's not about opposing the project to the landscape but creating its association to it, by means of the transformation process. In Venice, they accomplish this fusion by impregnating the architecture with the water.

These projects originate from the perception that the architectural product shouldn't concern itself with becoming a totemic object. It should have an attitude of "incrustation" where "the context is no longer idealized, conceptualized, or historicized. It is rather an under-layer of its own transformation. This is a political difference. The virtual instrument paradoxically becomes a principle of reality."

The project development and the final images were generated with the help of a specialized computer program that allows the fusion of several images. The resulting image incorporates all the information from the previous ones

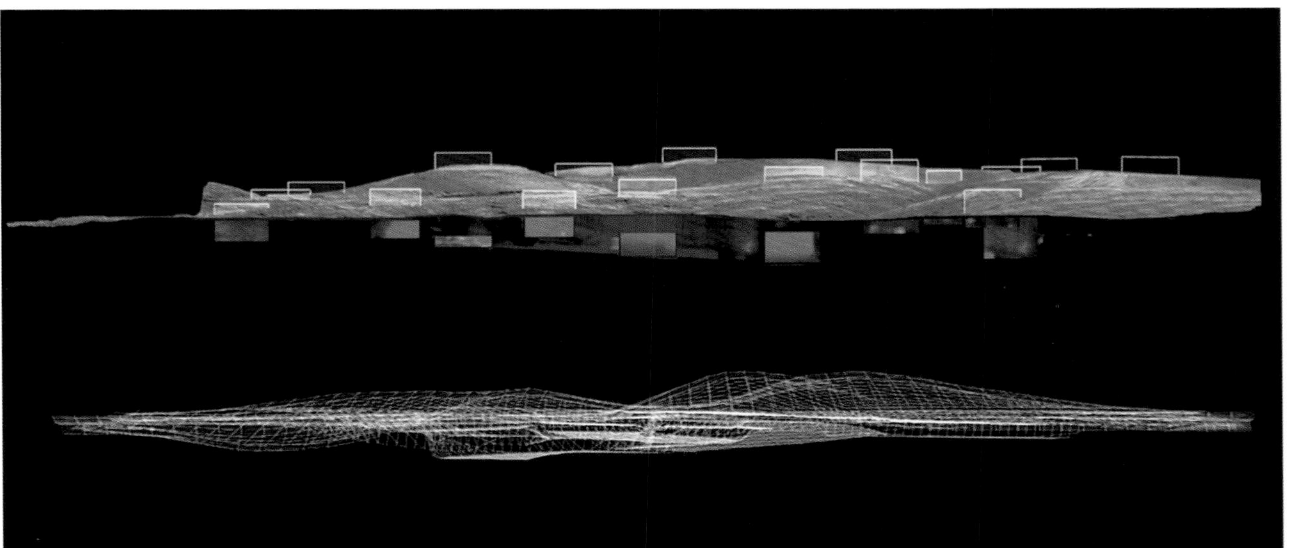

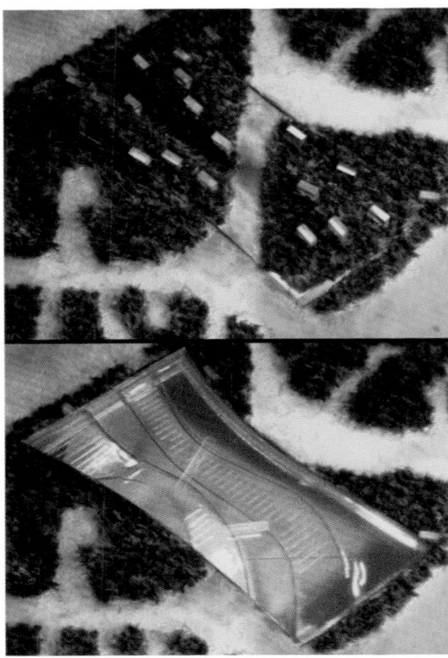

The Hector Peterson Museum is not just a construction project but the product of landscape deliberation and urban processes arranged to embed the different buildings within the site

venice cultural center

Roche, DSV & Sie. P

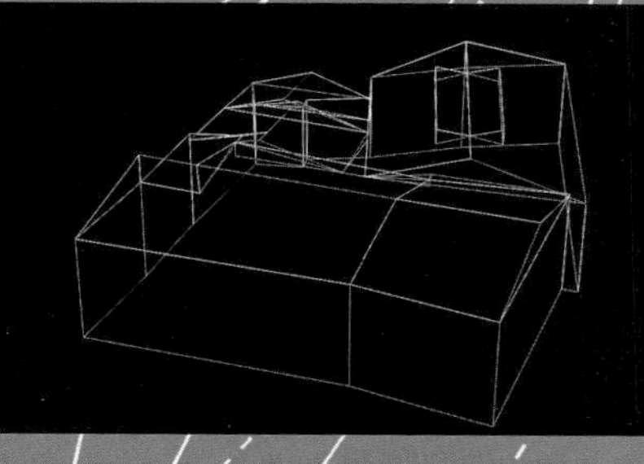

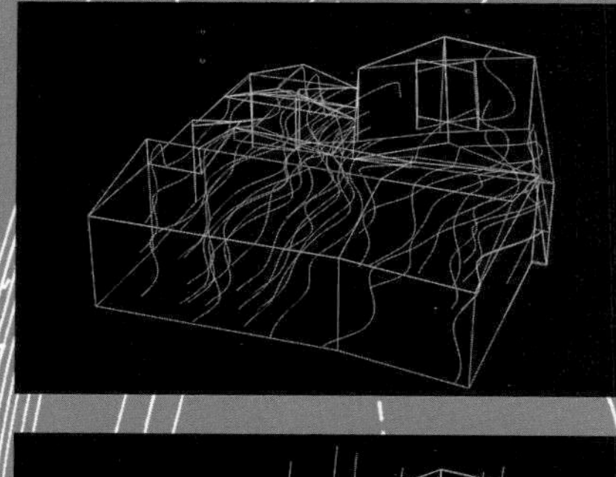

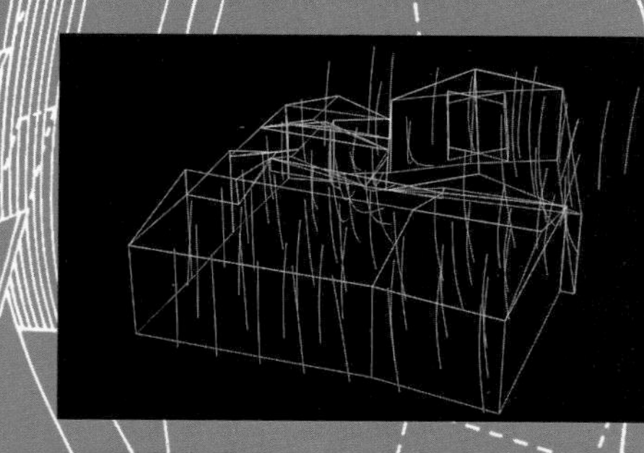

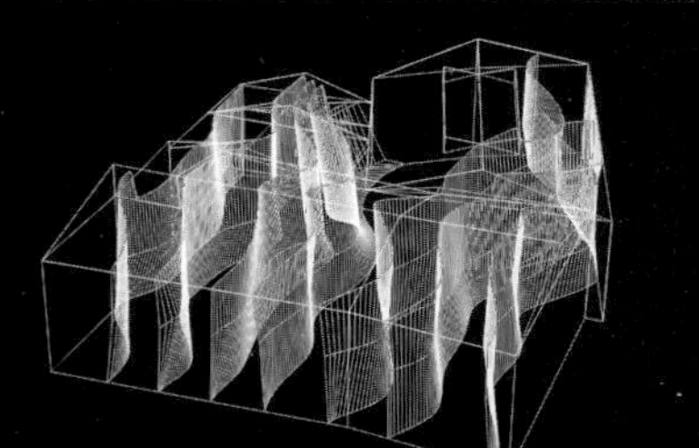

Location: **Venice, Italy**

Architects: **Roche, DSV & Sie. P**

Bovolo

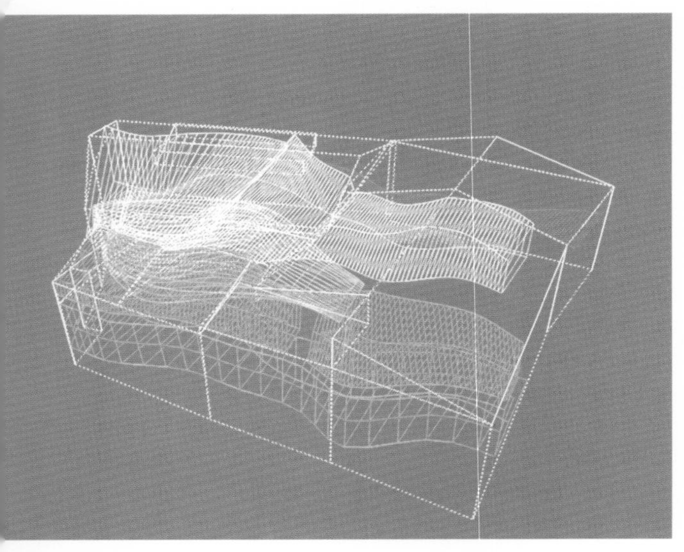

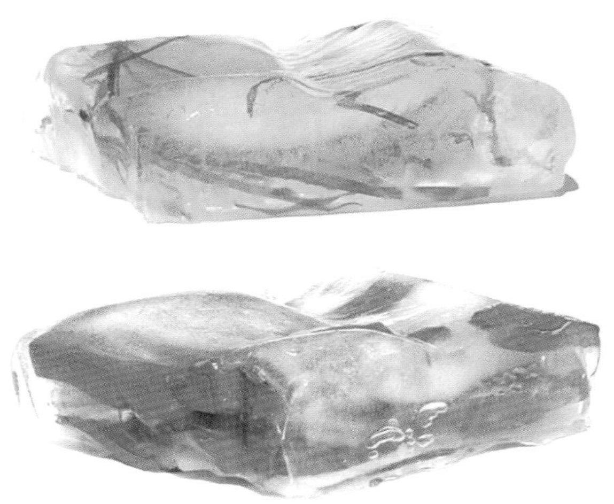

The project doesn't just lie on the site, but distorts it. The preexisting construction undergoes a mutation, metamorphosing into the final building. Placing the edifice on the site is not sufficient; attention is paid to the transformation process to determine its final shape

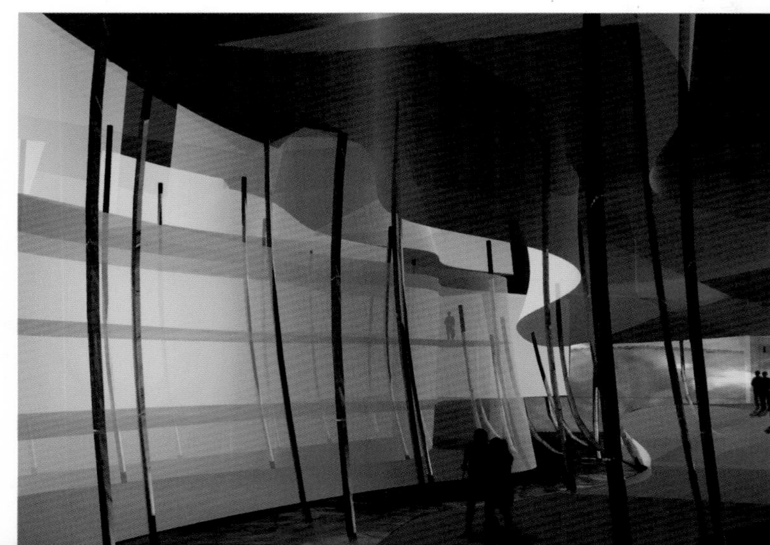

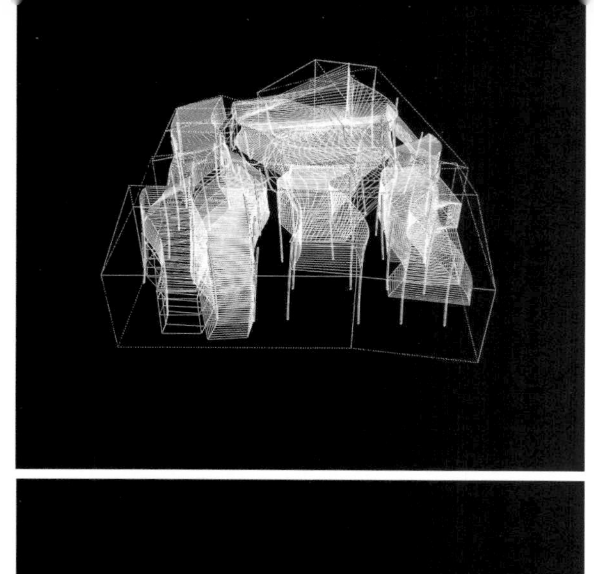

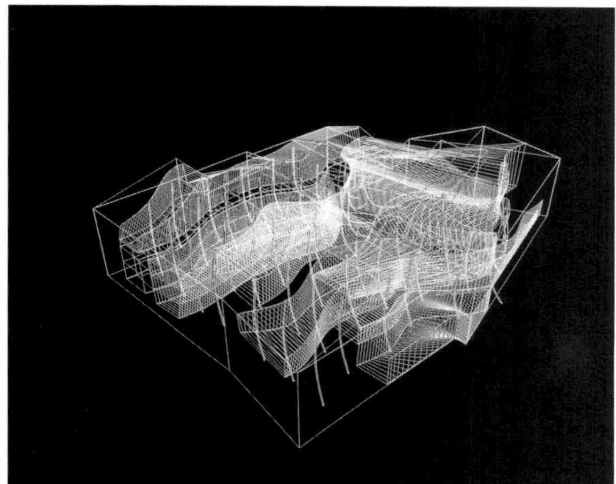

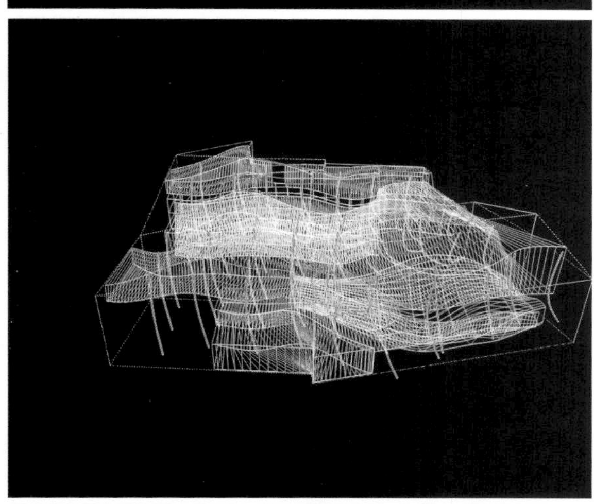

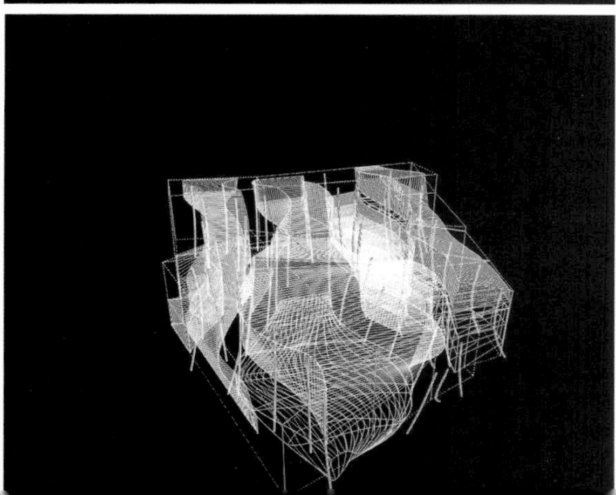